EMBROIDERY
AND COLOUR

Embroidery and Colour

Constance Howard

VNR VAN NOSTRAND REINHOLD COMPANY
NEW YORK CINCINNATI TORONTO LONDON MELBOURNE

Copyright © 1976 Constance Howard.
Library of Congress Catalog Card Number 76-10763
ISBN 0-442-23556-9

Printed in Great Britain.

Published in 1976 by Van Nostrand Reinhold Company
A division of Litton Educational Publishing, Inc.
450 West 33rd Street, New York, NY 10001

Van Nostrand Reinhold Limited
1410 Birchmount Road, Scarborough, Ontario M1P 2E7,
Canada

16   15   14   13   12   11   10   9   8   7   6   5   4   3   2   1

Library of Congress Cataloging in Publication Data
Howard, Constance.
    Embroidery and colour.

    Bibliography: p.
    Includes index.
    1.   Embroidery.   2.   Color in textile crafts.
I.   Title.
TT770.H68   1976   746.4'4   76-10763
ISBN 0-442-23556-9

Contents

Bibliography

Colour

The Art of Colour Johannes Itten, Van Nostrand Reinhold, New York 1962

The Bauhaus Thames and Hudson, London 1962

Interaction of Colour Josef Albers, Yale University Press, Newhaven and London 1971

Art and Visual Perception: A Psychology of the Creative Eye Rudolf Arnheim, Faber, London 1956; Berkeley and Los Angeles University, California 1966

The Principles of Harmony and Contrast of Colours M E Chevreul, London 1854; New York 1967

The Story of Colour from Ancient Mysticism to Modern Science Faber Birren, Connecticut 1941

Creative Colour Faber Birren, Von Nostrand Reinhold, New York 1961

The Textile Arts Verla Birrell, Harper and Row, New York 1959

Colour: Basic Principles and New Directions Patricia Sloan, Studio Vista, London 1968

Basic Design

The Dynamics of Visual Form Maurice de Sausmarez, Studio Vista 1964

Textiles Norma Hollan and Jane Saddler, Macmillan, London and New York (3rd edition) 1968

Dyeing

Fabric Printing and Dyeing David Green, Macgibbon and Kay, London 1972

Dyes from Plants Seonaid Robertson, Van Nostrand Reinhold

Vegetable Dyeing Alma Lesch, David and Charles, Newton Abbot 1970

Embroidery

Inspiration for Embroidery Constance Howard, Batsford, London 1966; Branford, Newton Centre, Mass, 1966

Experimental Embroidery Edith John, Batsford, London 1976; Branford, Newton Centre, Mass, 1976

Design in Embroidery Kathleen Whyte, Batsford, London 1970; Branford, Newton Centre, Mass, 1970

Metal Thread Embroidery Barbara Dawson, Batsford, London 1976; Watson-Guptill, New York 1976

Machine Embroidery: Technique and Design Jennifer Gray, Batsford, London 1973; Branford, Newton Centre, Mass, 1973

Patchwork Averil Colby, Batsford, London 1958

Quilting Averil Colby, Batsford, London 1972

Machine Embroidery Christine Risley, Studio Vista 1969

Pattern and Embroidery Anne Butler and David Green, Batsford, London 1970; Branford, Newton Centre, Mass.

Needleweaving Edith John, Batsford, London 1973; Branford, Newton Centre, Mass, 1973

Canvas Embroidery Diana Springall, Batsford, London 1971; Branford, Newton Centre, Mass.

Ideas for Canvas Work Mary Rhodes, Batsford, London 1971; Branford, Newton Centre, Mass, 1971

Canvas Work Jennifer Gray, Batsford, London 1971; Branford, Newton Centre, Mass, 1971

Encyclopaedia of Needlework Therese de Dillemont, Mulhouse, France DMC

Stitches

Embroidery Stitches Barbara Snook, Batsford, London 1972; Crown, New York

Mary Thomas's Dictionary of Embroidery Stitches Hodder and Stoughton, London 1934

Machine Stitches Anne Butler, Batsford, London 1976

Stitchery: Art and Craft Nik Krevitsky, Van Nostrand Reinhold 1966

Machine Stitchery Gay Swift, Batsford, London 1974; Branford, Newton Centre, Mass, 1974

The Stitches of Creative Embroidery Jacqueline Enthoven, Van Nostrand Reinhold, New York 1963

Introduction

What does this title conjure up? Tangled skeins of brilliantly coloured threads in a variety of textures or those in subtle tones, arranged precisely in their boxes, to be selected with care, the glint of metal threads, the glisten of sequins and beads, or the fascination of searching for exactly the right fabric from the wealth of colours and materials available.

From this wide choice it is difficult to select the right fabric and colour for a particular piece of work and to suit a specific idea which could be interpreted differently, according to the way in which the threads and stitches are used. In embroidery, colour may be exploited fully, which is one of the chief attributes of the craft, but preference for certain colours is highly personal; what excites one person may be hated by another, thus limiting experiment. Prejudice against certain colours is often linked with past happenings, as in childhood when these colours were associated with people, places and things which were detested. By understanding something of the psychology of colour some of the reasons for this bias could be removed. By learning about the reaction of one colour on another and by experimenting with those usually avoided, the fear of the unfamiliar colour scheme should vanish as should the avoidance of some colours.

The manipulation of cloth by gathering, folding and padding, also its light absorbency, affect colour. The overlaying with threads and the closeness or openness of stitches, the directions in which they are worked appear to change the colour of a background fabric and are the means of obtaining greater variety of tone with limited colours.

Few people have a natural sense of colour where the choice instinctively seems right. It has to be learnt by trial and error, by looking at nature, by writing down what is seen and by analysing why one scheme appears to be more pleasing than another. Children can put many colours together and they seem right, whether they are bright or subdued; adults often lose this ability and arrive at schemes they prefer by experiment, and by hard work, or play safe with conventional ones. By placing together colours not normally considered 'to go', by looking at everything from the colour angle, by choosing one colour and adding others from a large heap of fabrics and threads, then subtracting again until a personally pleasing scheme is arrived at, aesthetic appreciation of colour grows, as does the art of looking and 'seeing'. It is hoped that this book may help to eliminate a few misconceptions, without involvement in complicated scientific colour theories. If more detailed and advanced knowledge is required there are excellent books which deal entirely with colour theory and light with the additive process concerning the optical blending of light rays and the subtractive process in the mixing of pigments, some of which are listed in the bibliography.

Colour and Symbol

Colour affects everyone, some people being more sensitive to its influence than others. Itten in his book *The Art of Colour* explains the parts played by 'the physicist who studies electro-magnetic energy vibrations, measuring and classifying colours; the chemist who studies molecular structure of dyes and pigments, colour fastness and fugitiveness, synthetic and natural dyes; the physiologist who studies the light and colour effects on the eye and the brain, chromatic colour vision and after images; while the psychologist studies the influence of colour radiation on the mind and spirit, colour symbolism and expressive colour effects. The artist uses both eye and brain to discover the relationships of colour agents and their effects on man.'

Many experiments have been conducted to determine the psychological reaction of animals and human beings to different colours. These are still being carried out, and there is today a greater awareness of the value of colour in everyday life. Everyone has favourite colours and tends to use these constantly, perhaps being afraid to branch out into schemes which employ different colours in a more imaginative way. The unusual or unexpected combinations can shock. Some time ago, before colours were as boldly used as they are now, an experiment was carried out in a works canteen. Food served regularly was one day displayed on different coloured plates, starting with black through the dark to light colours, to white. The dark plates of food were ignored, while the pale plates and the white plates in normal use, were selected. This conservatism is still seen in the choice of beige or fawn as backgrounds for embroidery. They are safe but often result in dull pieces of work. Another experiment (carried out in the USA), concerned a publishing firm which decided after argument to produce a book with a white jacket. At the last minute it was felt that the choice was wrong, but coming to no agreement, a suggestion was made to produce the same book with different coloured jackets. Among these were white, yellow, blue, hot pink and lime; the sales results showed that white and yellow were least popular, hot pink sold well but blue was the favourite colour.

Everyday living is affected by colour. Posters and street advertisements attract by their strength of colour and tone rather than by their subject matter; interiors of hospitals and other institutions are often neutral or pale; green being a widely chosen colour as it is supposedly restful and has a calming effect. Red can irritate by its strength and insistence and can make some people ill. One red wall in a studio, otherwise white, created opposite reactions. One student said 'I love that red wall, it makes me feel warm and I can work harder', but another student had to turn her back on it whenever she was there; she said 'I can't stand that red wall, it makes me feel sick'. A cold, bright blue wall has been known to make people very depressed, in fact to make them physically cold in spite of normal temperatures.

Colour may be in the form of pigment, dye or light but all colours are relative to one another. Colour is reflected light which transforms the environment according to its source plus intensity. The Grand Canyon in Arizona, USA, looks scarlet and pink in strong sunlight, or purple, dark grey and foreboding in deep shadow. On a dull day things appear drab, greyish and cool, on a hot sunny day, colours may look paler, but shadows vary and may be blue, purple or greenish. The sky shows all colours from deep black, royal purple, through red, apricot and pale pink to green-blue and bright clear blue, all these colours reflecting onto the earth. A coloured object such as a shiny red vase or the surface of a piece of equally red knobbly tweed will vary in intensity with its reflective quality, also with the strength and position of the light, even if each is known to be of similar brightness. In relation to other red objects and textures or those of different colours placed with them, the vase and the tweed could appear to be duller, darker, shinier or smoother than when alone.

At present there is considerable freedom in the use of colour. Those restrictions that exist are often of ancient origin, such as the prerogative in the wearing of purple by royalty on the occasion of a coronation, a custom surviving from before the time of the Roman Emperors when red and purple dyes were difficult to obtain, extremely costly and therefore rare and exclusive. Significance was given to certain colours and still survives. Cardinals and judges wear red robes, and scarlet and gold costumes are worn by beefeaters at the Tower of London. Uniforms and their decorations have specific colours; academic robes with coloured hoods and costumes worn on certain occasions by civic dignitaries are of Renaissance or even earlier derivation.

The ancient laws of heraldry are observed still, and metal may not be placed on metal nor colour on colour. Heraldry as known today developed during the Crusades in the early thirteenth century, when the closed helmet required a man to have some means of identification, such as decorations on the shield, helmet and the surcoat covering his chain mail.

Ideas derived from heraldry are seen in striped scarves of schools and universities, blazer badges, flags pertaining to different nations and the striped ribbons accompanying military medals.

Colour symbolism in the Church is becoming less rigid and certain colours such as red, which signifies the Holy Blood, and the sacrifice of the martyrs once referred to a red on the crimson side, while green was a mid-green, and blue a cross between cerulean and ultramarine, but they are now less rigidly defined. Red may be vermilion, green may be yellower or bluer or darker as in peacock green, while blue may be more turquoise, or the rich colour nearer French blue. White may be woven with metal threads – lurex now – as may other colours. Today the decision is often left open for a personal choice to be made on the colours of vestments which are more expressive of the ceremony and of the setting in which they will be worn. Colours such as white and gold are often associated with certain feast days and festivals, while the more sombre colours such as browns, russets and greys are reserved for periods of penitence and mourning.

In different countries colours have diverse and often

conflicting interpretations, many of them having been handed down by the older civilisations where colour had much significance and symbolic meaning. This belief in colour symbolism has resulted in the perpetuation of certain customs and superstitions in the uses of colours on certain occasions. In China for example, white is worn for mourning and red for weddings where the colour plays an important part in the marriage ceremony as it does in India. Records show that in 1000 BC the Chinese used colours to denote certain elements; red symbolised fire or south, black was for water or north, green for wood and east, while yellow was indicative of earth and white of metal and mist; it was also the colour of good fortune. Yellow was an imperial colour which belonged to the Emperor in China. The Japanese emulated the Chinese Court customs in the seventh century AD and the male ranks of the nobility were distinguished by the colours of their hat cords, later by completely coloured hats. Red and yellow together are frequent in oriental symbolism and are seen in paintings, woven fabrics and in embroideries. Red in Asia is thought to give life, and babies are often clad in red garments. White is used for mourning in India and does not signify purity but death and the devil, while black is a non-mourning colour often the colour of children's clothes. In England white has become associated with weddings, christenings and confirmation ceremonies, while black and later, violet, have been the colours of mourning and half-mourning, but these customs are changing and now a variety of colours is worn on both occasions, perhaps modified at funerals. In the Old Testament the elements were suggested by blue for air, red for fire, purple for water and white for earth. The combination of these colours represented the presence of God. Some colours have strong pagan associations, such as yellow and gold, symbolic of the sun and worshipped by the Egyptians and the Incas whose lives were controlled by the Sun God who gave light and heat, without which no man could exist. Black was the colour of resurrection in christian Egypt, but often denoted evil, oppression, darkness, the opposite to light and was identified with witchcraft and necromancy in christian and pre-christian times. Some colours were supposed to possess magical properties and are still thought of by some primitive people as curing diseases. Amulets and gem stones of certain colours have been worn since civilisation began, to ward off the evil eye or to guard against ill health and danger. They are in evidence today, worn as charms and lockets by both sexes. Colours even in the fourteenth century were known to have meant opposite forces and could signify good or evil. They were expressive of different occurrences and moods according to the period, the people and the country in which the particular symbolism developed.

Superstition still exists and prejudice is found in the avoidance of certain colours, often based on old wives' tales, and sayings handed down from family to family, such as 'green is unlucky'. Green has many other attributes such as 'green with envy'; someone who can grow plants easily is said to have 'green fingers' (or in America 'green thumbs') but a person may be said to 'be green' who is unaware or inexperienced in some way, perhaps 'unripe'. White in some countries has denoted purity since pre-christian times when the Egyptians used pure white linen for winding sheets. It is also a symbol of innocence, 'as white as a lily'; while 'as white of a sheet' is still used for someone looking very pale or shocked. 'Blue with cold', 'blue stocking' – a learned lady – 'purple with rage', 'black as pitch' and 'as black as your hat', are still sayings in common use as are many other phrases all describing and associating colours with emotions, objects and situations of the past, which have been handed down to the present time, although their original connotation is lost.

Colour symbolism is a wide and fascinating subject, too vast to explain in detail in the context of this book; but an understanding of some of the meanings attached to its use is necessary when designing for ceremonial, heraldic and ecclesiastical embroidery. Titles of useful books are listed in the bibliography.

Colour and environment

Certain colours and signs are understood internationally. Red is a sign of danger; the red cross indicates medical aid; while red is associated with London buses although they are now occasionally covered in multicoloured patterns. Green implies safety to proceed. In Great Britain the flashing orange beacons at the black and white zebra crossings and the many, coloured road signs, are understood without written explanations being necessary. Combinations of shapes and colours which have meaning today can be found everywhere but some people seem unaware of colour unless it 'hits one in the eye' and is so blatant that it shrieks. The subtle gradations of pale skies, the fine variations in the greens of leaves or in the blades of grass or the many colours in a brick wall or a paving stone go unappreciated. In spite of this lack of observation there is now a greater awareness of colour and its stimulating qualities in comparison with the interest taken in it during the past. Ideas on the conventional use of colour have broadened considerably during this century and there is a freedom from the restrictions imposed by the Victorians, which is refreshing. Black or drab colours were considered suitable for everyday garments for both sexes. In the Edwardian era pale tea rose, beige and greys were fashionable colours for women's clothes, while now they wear what they wish. Most noticeably men's clothes have changed, especially for day wear and are now as colourful as embroidered garments worn in the reign of Elizabeth I. Recently brilliant colours and patterned fabrics of all kinds have been juxtaposed, sometimes successfully, sometimes in glaring, tasteless mixtures. Colours thought by the Victorians to be shocking and daring, such as combinations of blue and green or orange and pink, are now commonplace. Red, purple and pink are no longer taboo with auburn hair, while small children do not conform by wearing the insipid pastel colours once thought proper for the young. Instead they are dressed in bright or dark clothes, often patterned, which look most attractive. Fluorescent colours which 'glow' from a distance have proved useful for protective clothing in occupations where it is necessary for the wearers to be seen clearly; they have been used also for children's armbands and school satchels, affording some protection against traffic when crossing busy roads.

Bright, stimulating colour schemes now enliven both rural and urban environments where once there was drabness and a lack of colour. Houses and cottages of all shapes and sizes are being re-vitalised by gaily painted walls and/or woodwork. Some buildings are painted over completely and the pale pinks, apricots and whites fashionable in various parts of the country, look well both in the urban and in the greener rural settings. Other schemes such as harsh mauves, bright reds and fierce pinks seem out of keeping with their surroundings, but in spite of these lapses there has been a great effort to brighten the greyness of many depressing rows of identical homes, with colours which have transformed them into individual dwellings of distinction. A dullish climate tends to emphasise the harshness when hard, bright colours are chosen, whereas they would scarcely be noticed in a country with a hot, sunny climate, such as one bordering the Mediterranean where the sun tends to bleach out the strong colours. In some of the slum areas of New York experiments are being carried out to enliven these districts, the old tenement buildings being painted from ground to roof with bright, abstract designs, in the manner of large canvases, often with exciting results. Walls of bridges, also underpasses, both in Great Britain and in the United States of America, are being decorated with murals, although in Great Britain, to light upon a building covered in decoration is a more rare sight, causing comment. Some enterprising artists have painted patterns over their houses to the loud dissent of conservative neighbours, as again people stop to stare at new ideas. With more understanding of the value of colour and pattern in everyday life, perhaps carried out with greater subtlety, coloured and patterned houses could become an exciting feature rather than a novelty, particularly in new towns which often suffer from a lack of character and depth of colour, seen in the weathered buildings of earlier periods, in long established places.

Colour is swayed by fashion, what is in one year is out the next, bright colours giving way to dull, pale to dark tones and plain to patterned fabrics. Dyes and pigments are determined by a colour council and it is often difficult to obtain 'unfashionable' colours, both in fabrics and in pigments, the year after they have been popular. The solution is to dye fabrics and threads and to mix paint if particular colours are required. An interior scheme or an embroidery may be ruined if the colours and tones are higher or lower than envisaged in the original idea. Commercial dyes are obtainable with full instructions on mixing and applying them to different fabrics. These used according to advice given on the labels or pamphlets issued with the dyes, and with the knowledge of the constituents of the cloth or yarns being dyed, should give reasonable results. Vegetable dyeing when time permits and the ingredients are available, gives beautiful colours, often very subtle and never harsh. It is an art in itself and useful books are listed in the bibliography.

In the book *Textiles* by Norma Hollen and Jane Saddler there is a comprehensive list of textiles made in America with information on their manufacture and particular qualities. Fewer synthetic yarns are made in England but are within the scope of the list. Threads are structured as long or short staple, from 60 cm to 12 mm in length (24 in. to $\frac{1}{2}$ in.): wool, linen and cotton being in this group. Silk is the one natural filament thread, while synthetics may be filament or continuous strand in structure. Filament yarns and staple yarns are man made by different processes in spinning.

Norma Hollen and Jane Sadler suggest for testing fabrics for dyeing: unravel threads from the warp and weft of the fabric; if they have different textures they are probably different in structure. Tweezers should be used to hold the threads in a clear flame. Try burning each kind of thread several times, noting down these results to see if they are the same.

This test can save some disappointment as many materials

today are composed of part natural, part synthetic fibres and retailers not always knowing the composition of the fabrics cannot advise customers.

The following are standard tests and are to be found in books on dyeing.

Natural fibres

Wool burns very slowly. When removed from the flame the fabric smoulders for a very short time only. It smells like burning bones, leaving black blobs easily crushed.

Cotton burns easily and very quickly if kept in the flame. It will continue to smoulder long after the flame is removed and creeps in a thin red line across the fabric, leaving black edges.

Wool and cotton mixture burns fairly easily and smells of burning bones. It leaves black globules.

Silk burns fitfully, leaving globules of black, easily crumbled ash. It smells strongly.

Linen burns quickly with little ash.

Man-made fibres

Viscose rayon is man made but cellular in structure. It burns quickly with little remains of ash.

Nylon shrivels up and drops very hard globules which will not crumble.

Rayon acetate burns slowly and melts, leaves a crisp black edge.

Terylene – as nylon.

On testing fabrics if it is found that the warp and weft are of different fibres the dyeing can produce interesting results, one group of threads taking the dye while the other group does not absorb it.

Colour observation

Colour is a part of life. Perhaps we accept it to the extent that its subtleties are often ignored. Colour is delicate, sombre, bright, eye-catching and insistent, or drab and apparently unattractive; but a second glance at anything reveals more colours than might have been noticed from a cursory look. One way to see and to understand colour is to study natural form and to make written notes on what is seen, also to attempt to explain these colours in words. With coloured pens, pencils, pigment, or with coloured paper, or with scraps of fabric to match the written descriptions, draw or stick down these colours by the appropriate notes as reminders of both the tones and proportions in the colour relationships and the way in which they correlate to what has been observed. This takes time but develops an awareness so that eventually colours can be remembered without making notes.

Rocks and rocky landscapes contain almost every colour and as in the Grand Canyon described on page 10, these change with the light. Burnt sienna, red and yellow ochre, lavender and dark greenish browns are seen in the redder rocks while the greyer ones contain many tones of mauve and pinkish greys. A spring landscape with fruit trees in flower is exquisite with pale pink and white blossoms bright against the yellow green leaves, the dark trunks and the new green grass often bluer than the leaves. A field in spring can look anything but green, with masses of buttercups and daisies crowding together. A ripe cornfield can be ochre or golden yellow with spots of red and white, of poppies and moonflowers.

The sky and atmosphere change constantly with the water vapour which forms the clouds. Here they are white and grey but of many gradations, not menacing but buoyant against blue sky. Note the distant landscape merging into the sky, becoming greyer compared with the foreground which is sharp and definite. The mistiness of a summer day is worth analysing to find out what kinds of colours could best express such an atmosphere
Photograph by John Hunnex

In England where the days are often grey and the colours muted, very subtle tonal schemes are to be found. The sky can be a dirty yellow grey, making the bright colours look brighter and more intense, while a vivid sunset reflects across the sky to the east and onto windows which appear on fire. In fact the sky is worth studying as every day it changes, occasionally being a clear blue but unless the atmosphere is pure, the smoke of cities and the moisture content in the air, dilute the intensity of a really blue sky. Clouds are white to grey of every kind and change with the position of the sun; every colour can be seen in a sunset from pale greens and apricot to blood reds,

Cloud formations are fascinating and always changing
(a) Shows a stormy sky with vestiges of rain, wind and swirling clouds. Colours found in clouds such as these are often cool, diffused greys, pale to very dark, or in the evening have a warmer tinge when the sun sinks below the horizon
(b) Shows a calmer sky which might be seen in the morning or evening when the sun is rising or setting. The contrast between the clear blue background, pale pinkish or greyish wispy clouds and the heavier greyed ones is more clearly defined

opposite bottom
The horizon is hard-edged in comparison with that of the landscape and therefore appears less distant. This is emphasised strongly by the darkness of the rocks against the white foam of the sea. Merging tones give a greater sense of distance but the atmosphere in the photograph appears colder than (2). Analyse the tones to find out a way of expressing this hardness and coldness
Photograph by John Hunnex

golds and purple. This study of the sky would supply sufficient colour changes to inspire schemes for many pieces of embroidery. Notes on observations of a sunset were made which read – three greys, from very pale to dark colours of cloud; pale at the base, dark at the top. Orange gold and brilliant gold edges towards the base of clouds; small pale apricot and dull apricot clouds which merge into larger, greyer ones. All of these floating on sky of greenish blue to pale blue grey. These colours were put down in order of proportions, the greys being most important in area.

The seasons change and with them nature adapts from brilliant to delicate colour, from warm to cool colour. Write down some of the colours seen on walks, or one day try to find a particular colour in things such as red and its variations, then later try to find colours of fabric to match what has been remembered. Look at stones in water and the same stones when dry, put other objects in water and look at the difference between the wet and dry parts noting the change of surface from dull to shiny. Look at reflections in windows and objects in windows. In fact try to look as much as possible with the aim of finding colours under different circumstances and in all places, until looking at and using colours becomes second nature.

Banks of clouds with innumerable tones such as might be seen
(a) on a day of mixed sunshine, wind and rain, where the clouds are blown rapidly along, to reveal blue sky at intervals

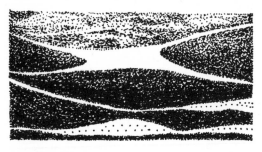

(b) breaking down cloud formations into pattern and tone. In the examples illustrated, French knots, line stitches and appliqué could be used to interpret these ideas in embroidery. Layers of coloured, sheer fabrics could be applied to a sheer white background as a border. On a larger scale the dotted textures could be worked on fine fabrics in satin or cretan stitch blobs, or in eyelets on the machine or by hand. Heavier embroidery could be worked in loops and rough textures on canvas

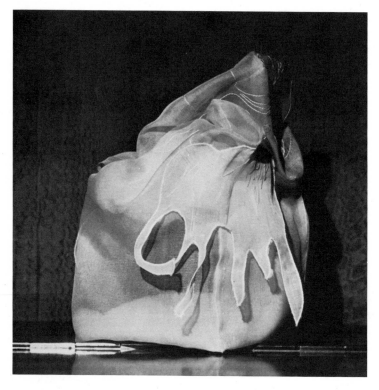

left
'Cloud Box' by Joan Schulze, California USA
All white, three-dimensional folded nylon, no padding. The contrast between the cut broken edges, stitched with a hard line, and the softness of the draped parts is shown in the photograph. The shadows from the freely hanging clouds add tonal variations to the structure

right
'Landscapes' by Mary Franks
Contrast of mood is expressed in colour. The landscape in each embroidery is taken from the same source. Above, the dark colours are menacing as if a storm were brewing. Below, there is a delicacy and light, with pale, muted colours suggestive of spring sunshine. Worked in hand embroidery, approximately 75 cm × 92 cm (29 in. × 36 in.)

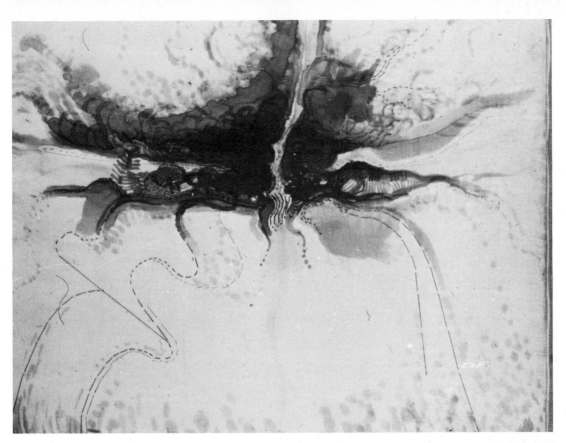

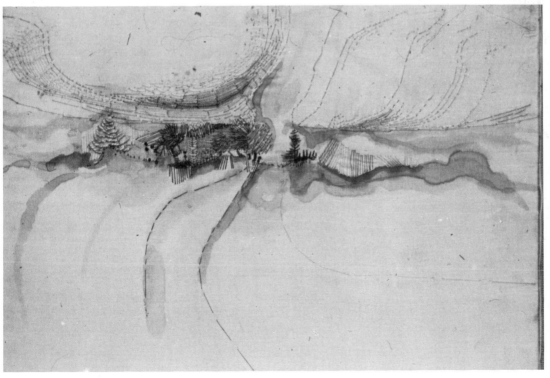

23

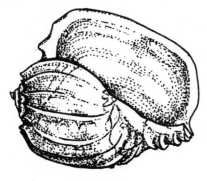

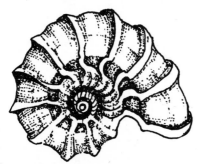

Drawings of the shell, illustrated in colour on the opposite page and described on this page. Only by careful observation can its details be recorded, such as its spines and moiré like patterns and its greyed, subtle colouring. It has the advantage of being small enough to hold in the hand. A great deal can be learnt about its shape by feeling its three-dimensional qualities with eyes shut. To draw the shell without having seen it, then to look at and redraw it is an invaluable exercise for anyone collecting ideas. It is noticeable that the pattern emphasises the shape. Details of its spiral structure are shown here

right
Front and back views of a shell from the Pacific showing beautiful, greyed, subdued colour, merging from one tone to another. The pattern consists of stripes of scallops between raised spines, melting into stronger, contrasting areas or burnt sienna and greyish cream
Photograph by John Hunnex

right
Design 35 cm × 29 cm (14 in. × 11½ in.) by Danena Wrightson-Hunt based on looking at a stone
Couched gold thread and silk on dark brown fabric. Some of the gold is couched with gold coloured maltese silk, some is sewn with coloured silks. The effect changes considerably according to the position from which the gold work is viewed, sometimes the gold is more noticeable, sometimes the coloured silks are prominent. The metal thread shines giving the effect of three dimensions. Concentrated areas of stitching as opposed to open ones add interest to the design
Photograph by John Hunnex

As an exercise in analysing colours in natural forms take as an example those found in a shell. First of all
(a) put down in words the colours seen
(b) try to find fabrics to illustrate the words
(c) use magazine advertisements to cut out the colours and the proportions of those seen in the shell. From this an idea could be translated into a design for embroidery, using both the shape, pattern and colours found in the shell.

In the shell from the Indian Pacific *Harpa davidis Röding* (illustrated on page 25), the outside colours are pale pinkish brown with creamy pink spines. The patterns between the spines or ridges are pale, mauvish grey with burnt sienna lines. Inside, the surface is very shiny, pale mauve grey, pale orange and cream with spots of burnt sienna on the edge of the lip. On the coiled part there are

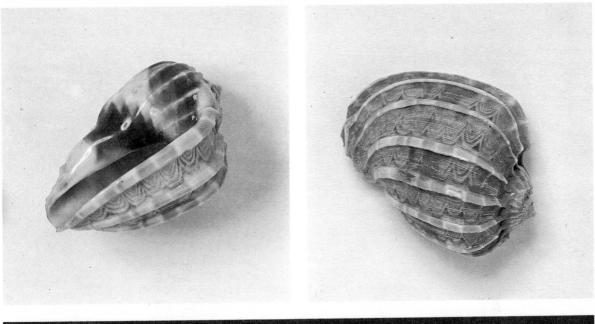

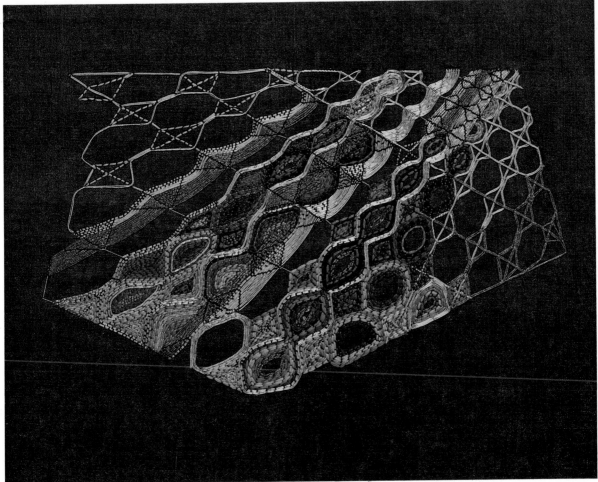

larger patches of burnt sienna, mauvish grey and pinky cream. In proportion, pinkish brown and mauvish grey are about equal and predominate. The cream patterns are fine and the burnt sienna inside the shell takes up about two thirds of the area in brown spots. This analysis can be tried whenever there is time and it will be found that natural forms usually contain colours that go with one another, also that it is easier to sort out those in static objects rather than in amorphous atmospheres, although each helps the other.

left
Ideas cut in paper, based on drawings of the shell. The tones could be translated into colours, either of one range or of different ranges and values. Transparency is demonstrated clearly here by tonal gradations of colour, the greater the number and the finer the gradations of tone, the more the effect of transparency will be seen. Stitches in gradated colours of threads or fabrics carefully dyed would be suitable for some of these patterns, depending on the scale and purpose of work.
An effect of transparency similar to that obtained by two overlapping different coloured tissue papers to make a third colour, is seen in the bottom

diagram. Try out a few ideas using overlapping coloured tissues, then put the resultant colours down in paint, finally working them in stitches. Couching would be a suitable method for developing some of these experiments, using opaque fabrics and threads to obtain an effect of transparency

right
Details of the same shell showing a side view with its delicate patterns. Enlarged they look like draped fabric. An idea could be developed from this set of details, using folded and stitched fabrics

OVERLEAF *left*
Part of an Indian hanging, in primary colours with bright pink and rusty red. The larger shapes of the animals with the small, fragmented patterns give liveliness. The black and coloured outlines emphasise the hardness of the shapes, the black ones thinning down shapes slightly. Rayon threads on a cotton background
Lent by Kay Cosserat
Photograph by John Hunnex

right
An Indian garment, showing strong contrast of colour and pattern. Circular cream flowers with mirror centres, are emphasised by an outline of black 'spots'. These spots are lines consisting of complete skeins of black thread, tightly couched at intervals and pulled out in bunches between the tying down stitches. This gives the appearance of spots which are raised, as are the red pompons, placed at intervals over the embroidery

Here the contrast of dark against light petals creates vitality. The light stamens surrounded by dark petals which become paler and increase in size towards the outside edges of the flower show tonal gradation. These could be reversed in an embroidery, using colours, to see the effect of dark outer surrounding petals fading to pale ones, but with dark stamens and centre to the flower
Photograph by John Hunnex

A beautifully veined leaf with a structure giving interesting shapes and a quilted effect. The light areas contrasting with the dark padded look, increase the feeling of depth. The photograph could be the basis of a design which is completely quilted, such as a hanging or bedcover, as the shape of the leaf and the facets created by the veins are related, although different in size
Photograph by John Hunnex

opposite
More patterns in cut paper, evolved from those on the shell. Again tones may be translated into appropriate colours in a number of different ways

OVERLEAF *right*
Banner 165 cm × 120 cm (4 ft × 5 ft 6 in.) by Constance Howard
Bottle green repp 'reflections'. Rug wools and tapestry wools in scarlet, orange and yellows with appliqué in purple and blue, in hand and machine embroidery
Photograph by Ione Dorrington

left
Part of a small hanging about 45 cm (18 in.) high by Betty Erickson, California, USA
It is worked entirely in satin stitch on scarlet and cream Welsh flannel, in crewel wools and perle. Most of the colours are greyed and light in tone, the green is acid and bright. Different colours in near tones closely juxtaposed create a rich effect, this being more noticeable in conjunction with the scarlet cloth in full, saturated colour
Photograph by John Hunnex

'Plant'. The leaves stand out clearly with their light edges, the ribbed surfaces giving an appearance of quilted fabric where the play of light and shade creates a quality of fine silk. Dark shapes with light edges are effective in a composition and can give depth to an embroidery
Photograph by John Hunnex

'Hollyhocks', an example of gradated colour, light to dark, leading to the centre of the flower, emphasising the concave three dimensional structure. The lighter veins appear as fine tucks and are raised on the surface of the petals. The colour of the petals is arbitrary, the variation in depth important in leading an insect towards the centre of the flower
Photograph by John Hunnex

Make a start by observing artifacts in everyday life, returning to natural forms later on. Look at solid objects such as rectangular boxes, at first in natural lighting then in artificial light, such as candlelight, which may be controlled to give many varieties of tonal effect. Knowing that the boxes are of a similar colour all over, note the tonal changes on each face, caused by the source and strength of light. A lamp or candle can be moved to give shadows and colour changes, lighter or darker than reality. Edges can be made to appear harder and to stand out, or softer, to merge into the background. Write notes on these colour variations and the results of changing the source and strength of artificial lighting compared to natural lighting. Your own observations will be of more value than reading theory. Look at 'box' patchwork and it will now be easy to see the reason for its name and how the three-dimensional effect has been obtained with the sequence of dark, medium and light tones of colour. From any angle these diamond shapes give a quality of depth, providing that the colours are arranged properly.

An experiment where colour and pattern can be a source of ideas, is to place plain objects in front of a slide projector; then to project different slides, trees, abstract shapes, people, patterns and colours onto the objects, which, according to their shapes, distort the images thrown on to them. A life model had thrown onto various parts of her body patterns from an old appliqué quilt, producing curved, distorted shapes quite different from those of the flat applied shapes on the original slide. The colour was subtle too as the model had darkish skin which produced

OVERLEAF *left*
'Garden patchwork' about
106 cm (42 in.) square by
Audrey Walker
Worked mainly in a variety of
tones of greens, concentrated in
areas to avoid spottiness which
occurs when dark and light
tones are placed at random. A
hundred patches of furnishing
fabrics, each 10 cm square, are
incorporated in the
embroidery, also applied lace,
crochet and surface stitching
Detail of stitches
Owned by Mrs Weston

right
Panel 76 cm × 91 cm
(30 in. × 36 in.) by Pamela
Whatmore. Natural linen scrim
over grey green fabric. Much
of the fabric has been removed
to give a fine net-like mesh,
mainly in warp threads. Behind
the threads a patchwork of grey
green, yellow and light olive
furnishing fabrics give a field-
like pattern. Diagonal lines of
stitching give strength to the
vertical lines of the linen. The
idea developed from drawings
of hedges, is delicate, much
simplified and has a calm,
peaceful quality of near tones
Photograph by John Hunnex

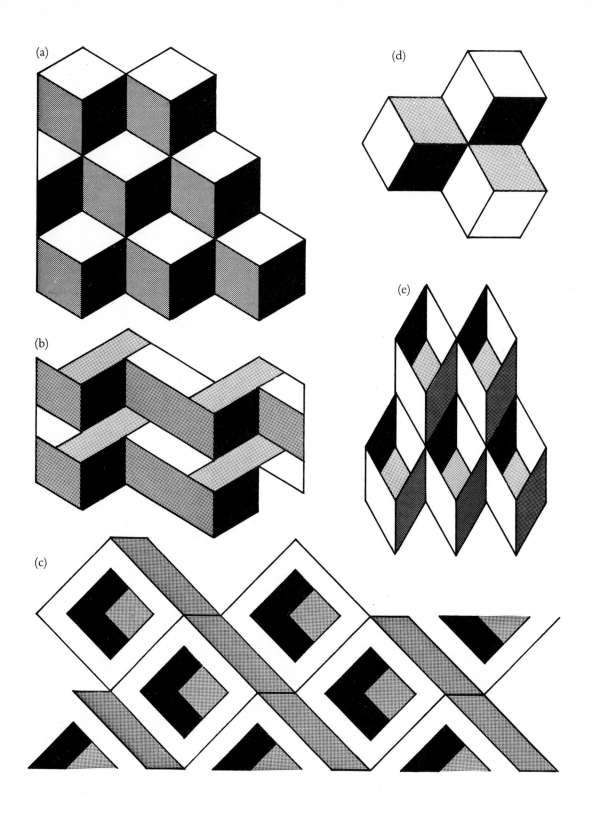

(a)

(b)

(c)

(d)

(e)

Patchwork patterns, all of which exploit apparent depth. They are self explanatory and groups of colours could lead to interesting results. For instance (e) could be worked in rows of gradated colours such as four yellows, four oranges, continuing round the colour circle. The same idea could apply to (c), the squares being divided by patches of mid-grey fabric

a richness rather than the brightness of the quilt. Many experiments can be tried out in this way, giving ideas that would be difficult otherwise to invent.

Other sources of colour combinations are to be found in museums where more time can be spent in study of immobile exhibits. In a natural history museum, colours and patterns of fur and feathers show fascinating qualities, often brilliant and sombre tones being juxtaposed. Crystals and rocks with their innumerable colours and facetted shapes are an inspiration for design that could not be created from imagination. Artifacts of the past can often start off a trend of thought leading to interesting embroidery, such as the study of decorated costumes of other countries, where differences and similarities of colour usage can be observed and noted down. In countries with a large peasant population colours are usually limited as the natural dyes are indigenous to particular areas; fleece is often spun and woven, undyed, producing cloth with patterns in tones, often very beautiful in comparison with the primary colours of dyes used for the embroidered decoration of garments and household articles, with red one of the most popular colours. More sophisticated and subtle colours are found in the embroidery of the court costumes of a country where there is also a large peasant community. Czechoslovakia and Hungary show a definite distinction where two entirely different kinds of embroidery have been developed.

Exhibitions of paintings of the past and of the present offer much thought on colour from which a great deal may be learnt, on the depiction of light, of depth of

OVERLEAF *left*
'The Creation' a double sided banner, 61 cm × 244 cm (2 ft × 8 ft) by Constance Howard
The colours are strong. The navy background symbolises night, the bright blue day, with the moon and the sun in yellow and red linen respectively. The crimson red of the square patches tie the blues together. The top panels represent the sky and air. The centre panels represent the earth and show free shapes, entirely hand stitched; one group on one side in herringbone, and the other one in cretan stitch. The bottom panels symbolise water, with reverse appliqué rectangles of cloth, in warm colours on the day side, in cool colours on the night side. Squares on the bias in blue, red and yellow cotton, some patterned, some plain, machine stitched round the edges in satin stitch in contrasting colours hold the panels together. Strips of patchwork round the panels and down the sides complete the banner. The contrast in both colour and shape of the patterns shows up well from a distance
Owned by Exeter Education Committee
Photograph by John Hunnex

right
A double sided hanging 1.83 m × 61 cm (6 ft × 2 ft) by Robert Moller worked on one piece of single thread canvas. The mottled grey ground in long, horizontal stitches gives greater brilliance to the orange and red of the cross shape, enclosing the dark and light mosaic like satin stitch patterns, which appears to glow. On the yellow the colours are less bright in contrast

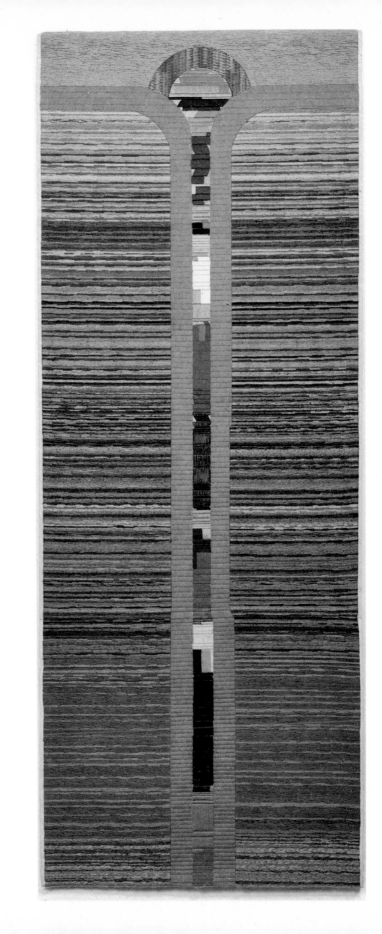

atmosphere, of the use of near tones and opposing tones, of pure colours used with greyed ones, of delicate tints combined with strong shades. Find out why one painting attracts, one is dismissed as uninteresting, apart from the subject matter. These queries, in time, will be solved by looking and thus increasing understanding.

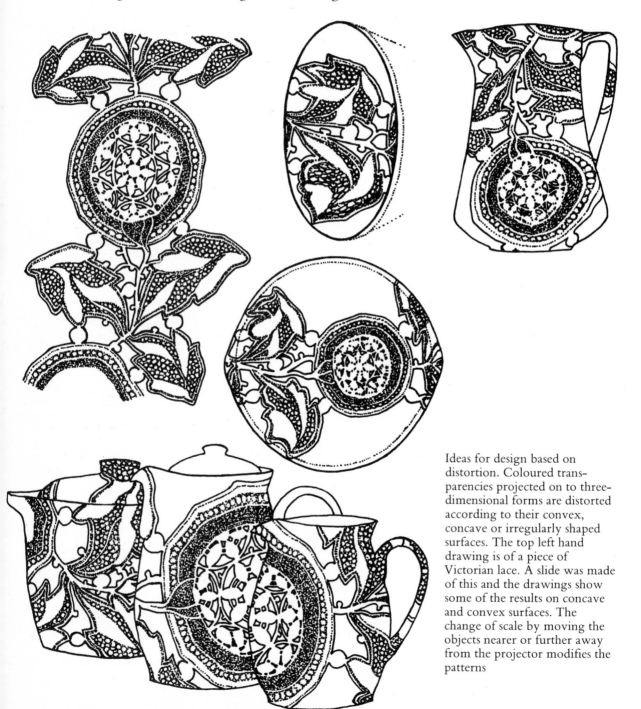

Ideas for design based on distortion. Coloured transparencies projected on to three-dimensional forms are distorted according to their convex, concave or irregularly shaped surfaces. The top left hand drawing is of a piece of Victorian lace. A slide was made of this and the drawings show some of the results on concave and convex surfaces. The change of scale by moving the objects nearer or further away from the projector modifies the patterns

Left: Flat patterns projected on to back views of figures where they are distorted by the forms which are mainly curved.
Right: Creating camouflage with transparencies thrown on to the figure. The results are dissimilar on the figures. The skin colour can change and the patterns can create bumps on smooth surfaces or hollows where there are none. Objects can be disguised in a similar way. The true colours can be changed and ideas for colour and design may be developed from this kind of experiment
Photographs by John Hunnex

OVERLEAF *left*
Front and back views of a cope designed by Ione Dorrington and owned by St Columbia's House. White Welsh flannel with applied silks; starting at the hem, ranging through yellows and reds to purple. The spaces of white between each colour add lightness to the whole concept
Photograph by Ione Dorrington

right
Chasuble by Ione Dorrington on a Korean shot silk fabric of brownish red and ivory, with appliqué in silk, ranging from purples to yellows. The shot silk was a very difficult background colour as the weave resulted in a pinkish fawn which changed with the light. Colours had to be selected for appliqué which were neither too deep nor too pale in tone. At the same time they had to look well from a distance
By kind permission of St Columbia's House
Photograph by John Hunnex

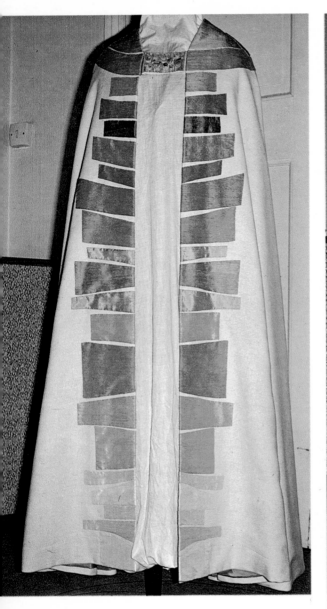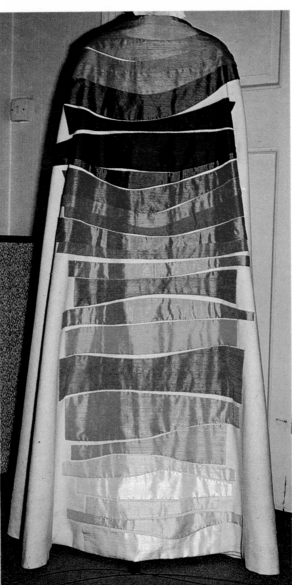

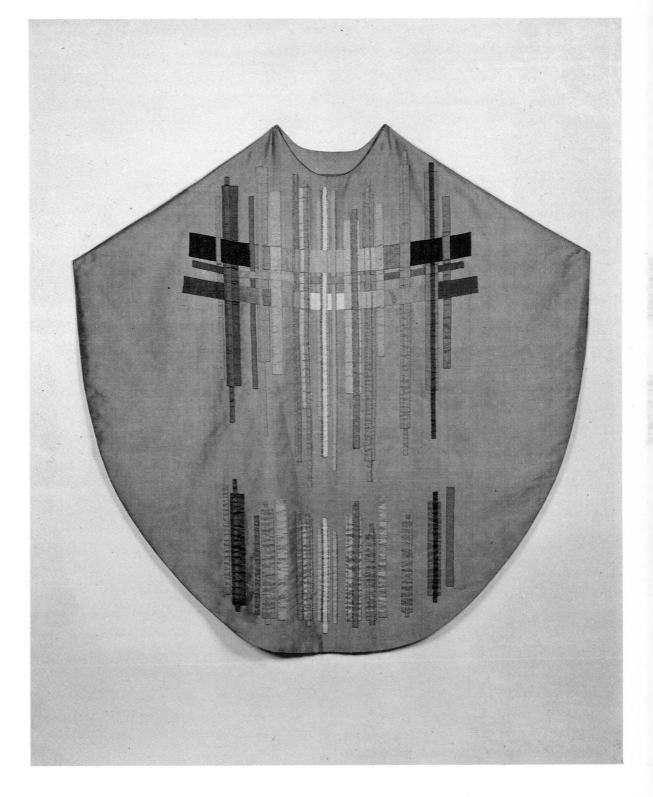

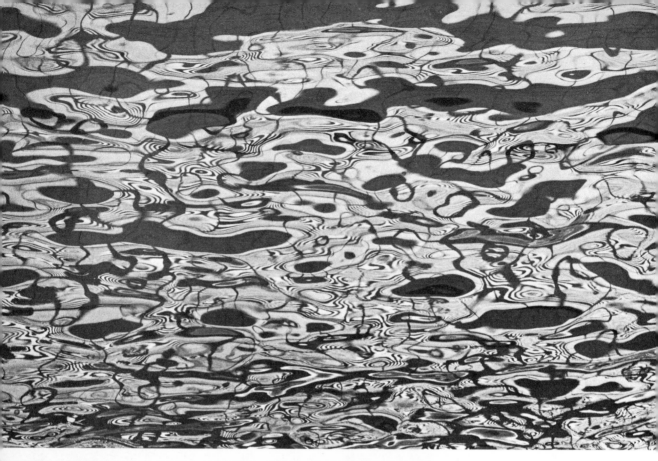

Fantastic patterns made by water in a pool. The variety of tones is strongly picked out and clear cut in the superb photographs, offering ideas on tones, pattern and colour for many embroideries. The diversity of line and mass is very definite; the ripples versus the splashing water are in direct contrast of tone to one another
Photograph by John Hunnex

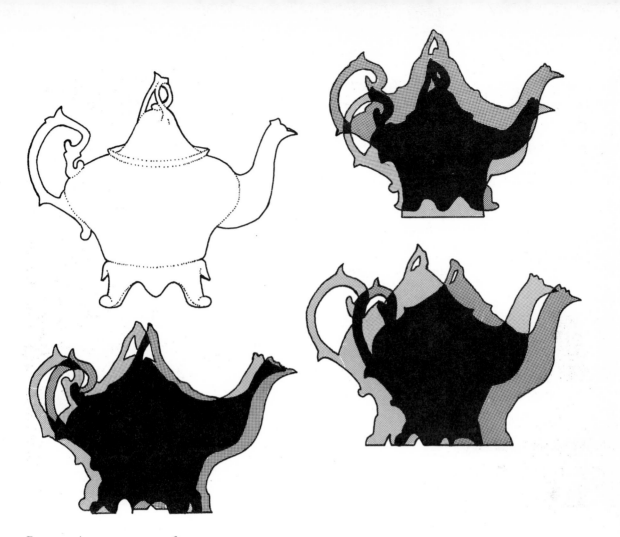

By arranging two sources of light to fall on one object, a variety of shadow lengths and widths may be made. According to the obliqueness of the light the shadows may be made narrow or wide and are a means of making interesting pattern in two tones. The object appears dark with the paler shadows surrounding it. In a human figure, the effect is rather like a skeleton with the definition of the flesh in the shadows made by the two lights, the pale wider shadows emphasising the apparent large fleshy part of the body. Amusing shapes occur when moving beneath two street lamps not too far apart, so that both create shadows

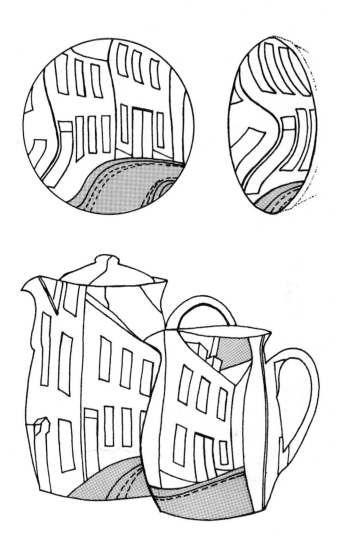

Patterns produced on curved objects, convex and concave, from a transparency of a street. By experiment with a projector many ideas will be found. Colours thrown onto coloured objects produce other colours, texture on texture gives different surfaces while the change of scale enlarges or reduces detail. A mixed collection of slides should be tried out as unexpected colours and textures could result, giving ideas for embroidery unobtainable in other ways. One transparency projected over another is worth trying

opposite
A detail of the altar frontal by Pat Russell at St Edburgha, Pershore Abbey
The background of blue fabric, with each colour superimposed, becoming brighter and lighter, create a strong feeling of depth. The lightest shapes of the book and the cross appear to leap away from the frontal. The whole effect is one of great depth and brilliance
Photograph by Pat Russell

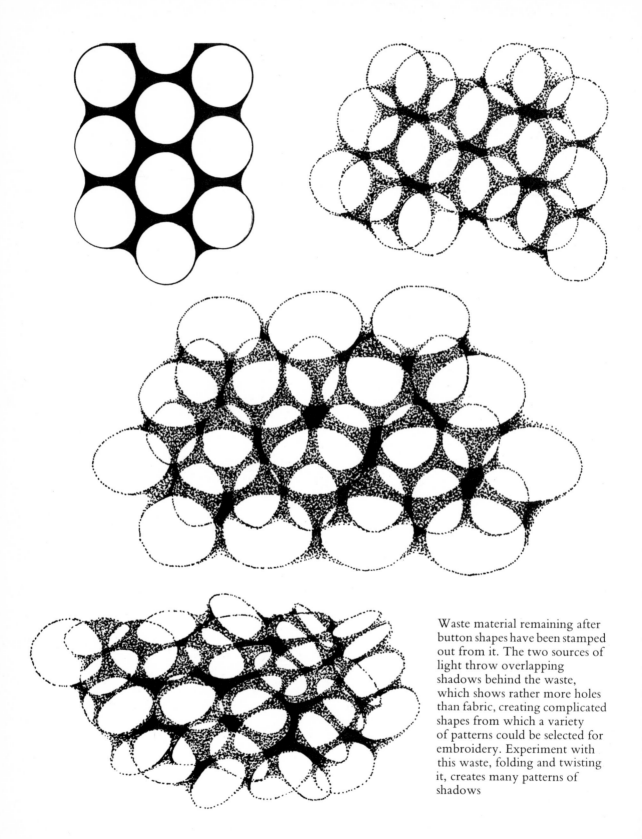

Waste material remaining after button shapes have been stamped out from it. The two sources of light throw overlapping shadows behind the waste, which shows rather more holes than fabric, creating complicated shapes from which a variety of patterns could be selected for embroidery. Experiment with this waste, folding and twisting it, creates many patterns of shadows

Reflections in metal and glass. The tonal contrasts are lively, breaking up the surfaces into interesting areas of mosaic like, fragmented pattern and tone. Reflections offer unending scope for design. By moving brightly coloured objects around, within the range of the reflective surfaces, many ideas on arrangements of both pattern and colour may be evolved Photograph by John Hunnex

Colour and embroidery

Although the use of colour in embroidery is the main subject of exploration, without some knowledge of design, both a good colour sense and technical ability will not improve a poorly planned embroidery. An appreciation of line and shape and some skill in putting down on paper ideas fostered from observation of things around us, is a necessary preliminary to most work. This may be accomplished by drawing or by manipulation of paper shapes, placing both lines and shapes together in a well arranged composition, for a definite purpose and within a limited area. The choice and use of fabrics and threads is a means of expressing individuality in the working out of the idea in embroidery.

There is a fascination, in fact an incentive to start work at once on seeing a bag of brilliantly coloured threads spilled out onto a table. Remnants on a fabric counter have this same effect and many of us cannot resist them, jumbled up in a heap, some drab, some bright, the kaleidoscope of colours and textures attracting us like a moth to a light. An intriguing part is in the selecting of fabrics from the heap, those with quality as well as colour from those less good, the price being of secondary importance when choosing colours, although a bargain adds to the excitement. This matter of selection is the keyword in design; in every way a personal choice is the basis of individual work. What is chosen and what is discarded or eliminated, from the inception of an idea to its fulfilment, results in an embroidery that is lively, original and good, mediocre or poor.

Large patchwork doll by
Roberta Roberts, California
USA
The arms and legs consist of
different patterned materials.
The dress is in varied sizes of
black and white stripes with
embroidery which also
decorates the arms. The hair is
of multicoloured wools.
The back of the doll is in
different colours from the front
but all colours are in strong
tones which go well together

Selection takes time and it is as difficult to know what to omit as to what to retain. Often at a remnant counter a collection of really super colours, textures and patterns of fabrics is made and laid carefully one on top of another. The fabrics look quite different from when mixed up in the heap, in fact they now constitute a personal choice. Someone comes along, looks at the heap and then if an eagle eye is not kept on them, the well selected and arranged remnants are 'swiped'. This emphasises the power and attraction of colour and the grouping of colours as against a haphazard jumble.

Natural and chemical dyes are the basis of the wide range

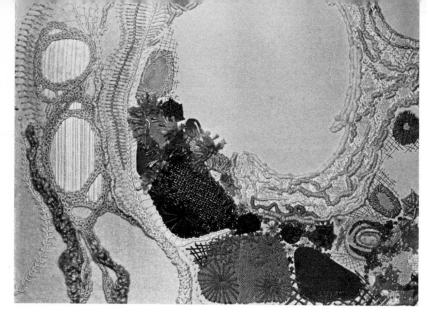

'Loam' by Susan Lyttle,
Los Altos, California USA
Fabric collage with stitches,
knotless netting, couching,
fringing and twisted threads.
Assorted values of off-whites,
pale oranges, pale pinks, light
browns and beiges are shown
on an off-white background
58 cm × 48 cm (23 in. × 19 in.)
Photograph by Marion Ferri

'Landscape' by Diana Harrison
A machine-stitched hanging of
dyed calico. The sky has been
spray dyed after crumpling up
the fabric. When smoothed out
an uneven, apparently bumpy
surface is simulated. The
foreground is bright, clear
colour, gradually changing
through the clear red to greyed
red until the distance is dark
brownish grey. The roundels
are padded with foam rubber.
Creased and dyed velvet cloud
shapes float, becoming smaller
as they disappear on the horizon
210 cm × 120 cm (4 ft × 7 ft)
Photograph Ione Dorrington

Patterned fabrics with embroidery. The shapes could be quilted on a plain background, or each set of patterns could be lined and padded so that they would be attached at the base of the work and free at the top. In choosing patterned fabrics to be placed together, a common colour should unite them, such as black or white in each fabric, or one colour, as near matching as possible. The scale of pattern would depend on availability of designs, but contrasting ones would give interest, such as very small with large, bold designs, or small squares with large circles.

Couching, stem, cretan and french knots could be used again in this embroidery

of coloured threads and fabrics used in embroidery in which colour is predominant. Monochromatic work relies more on the textures of threads and cloth and the choice of stitch which emphasises the design. An experiment worth trying is to take the same design, preferably small, and to carry it out in

(a) brilliant colours

(b) subdued colours

(c) all whites or all blacks

(d) one colour only on an opposite coloured ground

(e) tones of one colour.

Each piece will have a different quality, even when using similar stitches in the same areas of the design. Mood can be expressed in embroidery, both in the design and in the choice of colours. Again one idea can be embroidered in different colours to express

(a) gaiety – bright but not heavy colours

(b) seriousness – dull, subtle colours

(c) quiet – greyed but delicate colours

(d) clash – harsh, contrasting colours in their full strength.

Apart from designing on paper it is sometimes a good idea to work directly with the materials and threads. In this way as long as there is something to express, a spontaneous and often lively embroidery is created, but it is as well to remember that tones of colour are important too as with the use of bright, light and dark colours together, the proportions of each in a design can change its appearance. With colour, forms may be defined or concealed as by breaking up a form with a number of colours its true shape may appear to change, according to the placing of the tones and the sizes of the areas covered. In camouflage by painting vehicles, buildings and clothing of soldiers in small areas of colour suggestive of the environment in which they are stationed, the true shapes are broken up to become indistinguishable from the surroundings.

Colour choice is highly personal and it is difficult to remain impartial to schemes in which colours are disliked. One person may prefer an arrangement of muted tones while another will choose strong, harsh colours. Each scheme may be good of its kind and equally successful, but some knowledge of colour behaviour may result in an appreciation of both schemes even when a preference for one remains. This understanding could lead to experiment with more exciting and unusual combinations of colour to

A detail of 'Marigolds van Gogh-Go' designed by Doris Hoover, showing contrasting textures of coarse and fine fabrics, patterned and plain, in butcher linen, mexican cotton, linen, plain and hand printed. The frayed edges, loose stitches and ruching give a three dimensional accent and vitality to this work
Owned by Mrs Carl Beyer
Photograph by Marion Ferri, California, USA

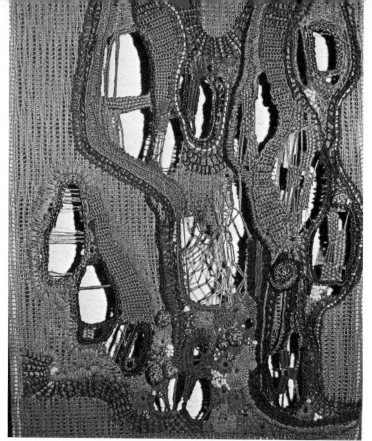

'Contretemps' by Bea Miller,
Los Altos, California USA
Pulled and drawn threads form
a loosely woven fabric, with
crochet, macrame and needleweaving. Purples, magentas,
pinky orange and small, dull
turquoise accents are worked
on a dull ochre background.
Crotcheted balls are embedded
in raised stitches 58 cm × 83 cm
(23 in. × 33 in.)
Photograph by Marion Ferri

'Iceland Poppy. by Bea Miller,
Los Altos, California USA
Stitchery and fabric collage,
stuffed, stitched and tucked.
Red-orange, yellow-green,
green-yellow, dull purple, and
burnt orange are seen on a
clear, light yellow-green firmly
woven cotton fabric
81 cm × 70 cm
(32 in. × 27½ in.)
Photograph by Marion Ferri

obtain greater brilliance, delicacy, contrast or depth.

In embroidery the texture of the cloth, together with the thread and stitch, affect the colour. In a natural form the colour is often a part of its structure such as the stripes in a piece of malachite or the patterns of shells; in an artifact the warp and weft of a fabric, perhaps in different colours, is structural, so is the colour of a plastic utensil; but colour may be on the surface only as in a printed pattern on cloth or an engraved transfer on a plate. In embroidery the stitches may integrate with the cloth or are superimposed onto its surface according to the way in which they are worked. For example, in needleweaving the embroidery thread becomes a part of the cloth as it does also in pulled work.

Materials are affected to a greater or lesser degree by the intensity and the angle at which the light falls on them, the colour changes depending on their textures, dull plain fabrics remaining fairly constant while shiny surfaces such as satin, plastics and those with a definite pile similar to face cloth, some velvets and corduroy velveteen, change perceptibly. The shiny surfaces appear darker or lighter than they really are, the pile fabrics change according to the way in which they are used. When vertical they look darker with the pile going up, and, when horizontal, they look lighter. In designing with these fabrics interesting patterns may be obtained by placing shapes in reversed pile to give two tones of colour.

Detail from 'Iceland Poppy'
Stuffed and tucked iridescent green taffeta, net and appliqué
Photograph by Marion Ferri

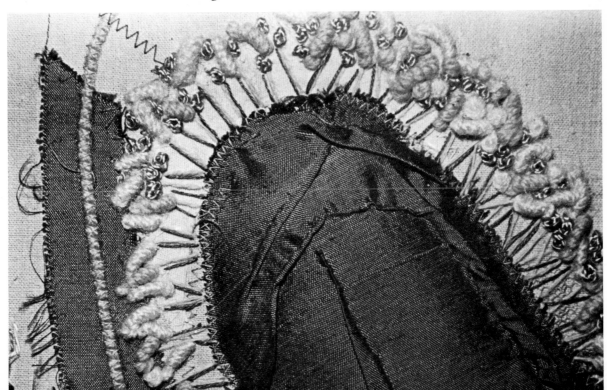

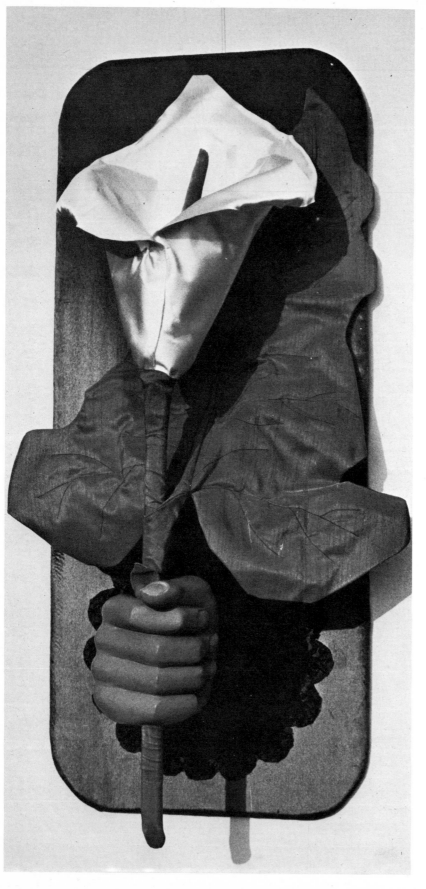

A striking contrast of tones and textures gives impact to this three dimensional panel by Eirian Short symbolising 'death'. The lily is lined and is in thick, white satin, about life size, the leaf is of a slightly duller green fabric. A white plaster hand is surrounded by a black lace sleeve. Machine stitching emphasises the veins. The upward thrust of the lily with its yellow pistil is very dramatic, all other colours being greyed or neutral

Photograph by Denys Short

Velvet

Velvet tends to overshadow other textures as it has a richness and strength not found in flat fabrics, it is therefore advisable when using it with other fabrics in embroidery, to place the work in the position in which it will be seen when finished. The velvet appears different in tone when vertical from when it is lying flat on a table, as the light falls at a different angle.

Exercises Using velvet or corduroy velveteen to make small patchwork patterns with the pile placed up and down and diagonally, give interesting results in tone.

(a) Use one colour of velvet, the design to be made up of shapes such as squares, rectangles or others which fit well together, to make an area of pattern in which the tones vary in depth. The velvet may be sewn or stuck over thin card to avoid clumsy edges, the pieces being sewn together as for patchwork.

(b) Use corduroy and velvet, of similar or different colours but equal in tone value when the pile is placed all one way. Cut out shapes, mount them and arrange to give a pattern of light and dark areas which can be mounted on another kind of fabric.

A border showing different directions of pile, using corduroy and velvet. These fabrics laid with the pile up, give lighter tones, with it down, darker ones, and diagonally again slightly different ones. This is a basis for dress decoration using self colour and self fabric in an interesting way

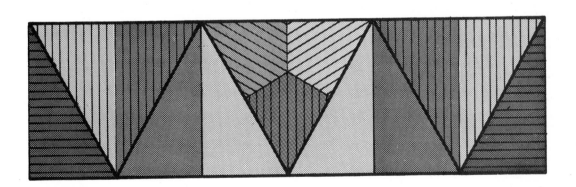

Patterned fabrics in different tones, used together, some bold, some fine in scale. The arrangement of squares and parts of squares on the diagonal gives an appearance of over-lapping shapes. Contrast between dark and light shapes, solid pattern and open pattern give liveliness to the whole idea which could be repeated on a larger scale.

Couching, stem stitch, whipped stem, running, French knots and woven wheels are used in the embroidery

A design using velvet and cloth together, with embroidery. The white indicates the background in a dull surfaced fabric. The light grey is a velvet with the pile running up. The dark grey is the velvet with the pile running down. This would indicate a velvet placed horizontally as on a bed. Cretan stitch, couching and double knot stitch are used in the embroidery. Where the velvet shape meet with the pile going in opposite directions they are overlapped, with the darker over the lighter edges. The velvet is more easily handled if mounted over card if to be part of a fairly flat hanging. For dress or to give a softer effect, it can be mounted, with the edges turned over vilene and sewn down with herringbone. One colour of velvet, with a variety of threads related to the colours of the fabrics would give sufficient interest with the textures of the stitches employed

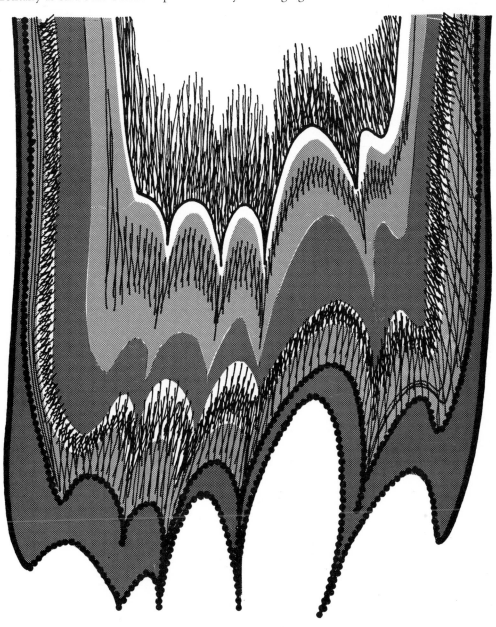

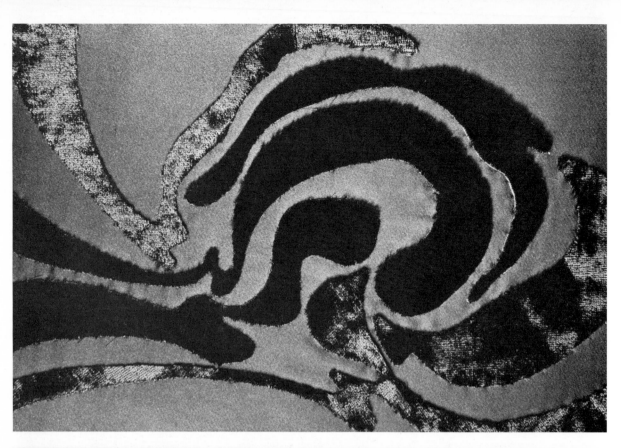

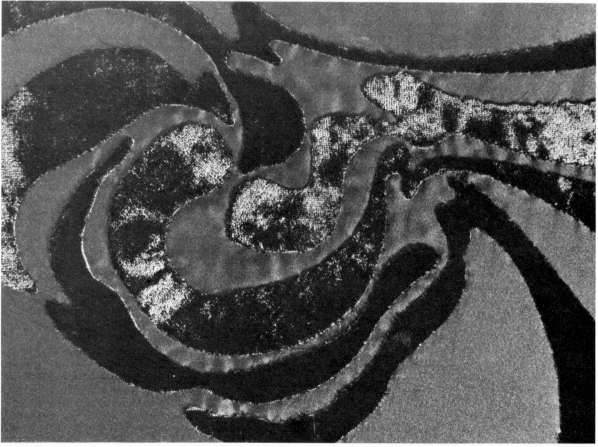

Black panne velvet appliqué on black wool. The example by Valerie Mosley is photographed under the same lighting conditions, but by turning them round the opposite way the pile appears different, the tones changing with the new direction in which the pile is laid.

Designs worked out in a pile fabric, in one colour only, but turning the fabric round, are a means of decorating costume, as with the shift of the weave the light catches the pile to give subtle variations of tone

Photograph by John Hunnex

Shot silks

Shot silks with the weft of one colour and the warp of one or more other colours are tricky to use, the sheen on the surface of the silk and the differences in the colours of the warps and wefts change the tones whichever way the fabric is hung. One colour dominates, according to the position of the light; sometimes the warp, sometimes the weft. Some shot cottons have similar properties but are not shiny. If small pieces of shot silk or cotton are shifted by careful control, from the vertical to the horizontal and back round to the vertical again, the tone and the colour of the fabric changes with each shift. The full beauty of this arrangement is judged better from a distance and changes according to the different positions in which the work is seen.

Designs in which fabric only is used, manipulating it to give tonal changes, can be subtle in the slight movement from the vertical to the horizontal direction of the warp threads. Embroidery to enrich these shot fabrics should not be too elaborate as the qualities of the weave are interesting alone, and added threads often superfluous.

To continue the exercises which show qualities of materials, apart from embroidery

(c) Use a shot material, a silk if obtainable or a furnishing fabric if this is more easily available. Cut out squares about 38 mm ($1\frac{1}{2}$ in.) in size. Make a pattern by arranging the squares in reverse, sometimes with the warp horizontal and the weft vertical and vice versa. Embroider as required.

(d) Cut out a number of similar squares, moving each square slightly at an angle, and inclining more until the horizontal top edge becomes the right, vertical edge. Note the change in colour from the first square to the last one. Six squares should be sufficient in one row to see the colour change. More squares or circles or other shapes may be cut and by manipulating them, interesting patterns arranged, which may appear dark going to light from the centre, or the opposite, a number of shapes placed with the fabric in one direction only, with a few shapes placed at a different angle, will show up the differences in the colours of the shot fabric.

All examples of design in which fabric is manipulated to vary the direction of pile, or the colours of warp and

Diagrams showing the direction
in which pieces of shot silk or
cotton may be manipulated to
give changes in colour and tone.
The straight lines are on the
grain of the fabric. Any design
incorporating this idea should
be tried out first of all with very
small pieces of fabric, which
must be seen vertically, if to be
hung finally in this way, as the
colour changes when vertical
and looks different again when
lying flat on a table

In this design, stripes are
incorporated with plain fabrics
and embroidery. Two different
striped fabrics are applied to a
plain background, some stripes
are cut up and shifted to give
different effects. Line stitches or
couching, running and French
knots are worked for the
embroidery. As in the previous
diagram fabrics can be overlapped, such as the white over
the grey, over the plain stripes,
over the grey, over the fancy

stripes. Card or vilene can be
used as a base for mounting the
fabrics, according to the purpose
of the work. Some shapes could
be padded if wished

weft, should be hung up from time to time as both the movement of the warp and weft of the fabric and the source of light will affect the colours before embroidery is worked on the surface. Rough textures such as knobbly woollens, furry fabrics, those woven with straw or cellophane, or with plastic threads simulating metal ones are all affected by light particularly with shiny and dull areas interchanging; the more glossy the fabric the more varied the tones. Semi-transparent and transparent fabrics such as organdie, terylene lawn, muslin, organza and chiffon look different placed in front of or behind light; in front of a lighted area they appear more translucent. By overlaying sheer fabrics such as chiffons, nets or gauzes in several layers of different colours, exciting, often unpredicted colour effects result. Olive green chiffon over shocking pink produces a rosy bronze pink, brilliant pink over mid turquoise produces a slate grey, turquoise over pink gives a greenish grey. Appliqué in opaque fabric of one colour on transparent backgrounds which are composed of several colours can be effective and gives the appearance of more colour in the design than is actually there.

Transparent fabrics

An experiment in which transparent fabrics were placed over a print in large areas of bright royal blue, scarlet, magenta and red violet, resulted in some interesting colour combinations.

(a) Light bottle green silk organza changed the colours and
    the blue became more brilliant peacock green
    the red became burnt orange
    the purple was almost black.
    the magenta became dull crimson

(b) bright cold pink chiffon changed the colours and
    the blue became bright violet
    the red became rose pink
    the purple became paler, to lavender
    the magenta became brighter and a lighter pink

(c) with overlaying in black organza
    the blue became navy
    the red became dark tan
    the purple became very dark, greyed violet
    the magenta became brown.

By overlaying several transparent fabrics in a different

Fabrics such as those with stripes and checked patterns have many possibilities for manipulation into other patterns. Bold stripes in two colours are best to try in the beginning. If black and white striped fabric is used a 13 mm ($\frac{1}{2}$ in.) stripe is wide enough for small samples, where parts of both black and white stripes may be blocked out with the opposite colours of thread to break up the hardness and to give more texture to them. Stripes embroidered in the opposite colours, such as working on grey and white stripes, with white on grey or grey on the white in narrow lines or in solid blocks, changes the appearance of the original fabric. By cutting striped fabrics up and re-arranging them quite complex designs may be made, particularly on a large scale. Fabrics may be cut up to make stripes as in patchwork, with lighter or darker tones of narrower stripes applied to the wider ones to give depth. Real depth by padding some of the stripes and embroidering others could also be tried out. Experiment with stripes is endless and intriguing and can lead to exciting colour combinations

69

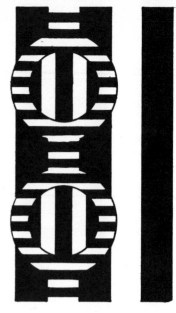

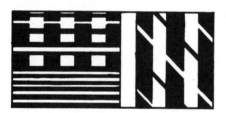

More striped patterns, some broken up with embroidery, some applied. Various widths of strip used together. A third tone introduced with these stripes, or new tones added, would avoid the sharpness of black and white.

By folding striped fabric, then recutting it, new ideas may result which are the basis of different patterns. The more colours in a stripe the more difficult it is to manage. Embroidery can be used to block out areas of colour whenever required so that the patterns and colours change. When necessary, some stripes may be folded to eliminate colours in parts only

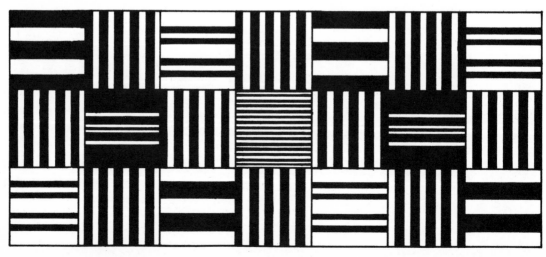

'Stoney Path' by Kathleen Smith
Part of a large hanging on a
grey hessian (burlap) ground
covered in appliqué shapes of
grey-blue velvet and green-grey
woollen fabrics. The stones are
made from nylon stockings in
various greys and fawns, padded
with white terylene wadding.
The flowers are in folded
chiffons in pale yellows and
apricot. Machine-embroidered
leaves on nets, leather and felt
fronds in apricot, yellow-green
and blue-grey are all raised, on
the varied green woollen tufting
of the grass which contrasts
with the delicacy of the colours
and textures of the flowers
Photograph by John Hunnex

order the resulting colours may be varied, according to which is over which. Opaque with sheer fabrics are effective, such as white organdie over white satin or black over black, or brightly patterned fabric overlaid with one of the colours in the pattern. Double layers of organdie, black with white or two similar colours put together are also effective. For these combinations of two fabrics the designs are tacked (basted) round the edges which are then stitched over by machine with a small zigzag or a straight stitch, or by hand with running stitches; the surplus material being cut away, to leave either the pattern or the background in the double fabrics. It is advisable to leave about 3 mm ($\frac{1}{8}$ in.) outside stitches other than the zigzag. By trying combinations of colours, quite striking effects are obtainable and with stitches added, to show through from both sides, the possibilities are many. Curtains, screens and special occasion clothes could well be decorated in some of these ways. Where small areas of light are required to gleam through the fabric decoration like pin points, a layer or several layers of opaque fabrics placed over transparent ones, with areas of these cut away to the sheer background, are a source of ideas and can be the basis of designs for screens, curtains and room dividers. Simple patterns requiring the cutting away of parts of the overlaying fabrics may be designed on sheets of tracing paper. The edges of the fabrics are more quickly machined over with narrow zigzag or satin stitch or they may be turned in when convenient and slip-stitched. The light filters through the sheer fabrics making this method suitable for lampshades. One idea which proved attractive and practical was an arrangement in strips of several brightly coloured chiffons overlaid with a fine, mid-grey cotton fabric. Small, irregular shapes were cut out of the cotton to reveal the different chiffons which appeared like jewels when lit from behind.

Mexican embroidery 64 cm × 56 cm (25 in. × 22 in.) in satin stitch, in primary colours of green, red and yellow with dark blue. Spaces and patterns are equally distributed over the background. The drawing is naïve but vitally alive and full of amusing forms. Tones are perhaps monotonous in their similarity
Photograph by John Hunnex

Shadow quilting and tone

Shadow quilting in which very brightly coloured felts are sandwiched between two sheer fabrics gives a delicate or a rich effect according to whether black or white organdie is used. The patterns are cut out in felts which have a thickness thus giving a slightly padded look; the

Mid Victorian embroidery.
A triangular fischu in
handkerchief linen embroidered
in fine white thread in padded
satin stitch, eyelets and whipped
outline stitch. The flower
centres are filled with openwork.
The charm of this work is in
the contrast between the fine
fabric and the solid stitching
which makes colour unnecessary.
The filigree effect of the fern
like leaves with the padded satin
flowers enhances this contrast of
delicacy and solidity
Photograph by John Hunnex

right
Black felt between two layers
of white organdie secured with
running stitches round the
shapes making both sides alike
with the felt giving a slightly
raised quality
This is an example of shadow
quilting by Valerie Mosley
Photograph by John Hunnex

OVERLEAF   *left*
4 scales of colour to give
gradations
(a) by mixing white pigment
with black to obtain an
achromatic scaled group
(b) black sheer fabric is placed
over a neutral fawn, each block
having an extra layer of the
black fabric until eight layers
give dense black
(c) slightly greyed blue threads,
arranged in sequence. The
photograph tends to darken
the darker colours but the fifth
colour is slightly darker than it
should have been. The threads
are manufactured, but to get
exact gradations dyeing is the
the best way in which to obtain
them
(d) a scale using fabrics which
are greyed, except for the pure
turquoise which is out of scale
and in the wrong sequence.
The second colour from the

light one showed the third,
slightly less green and the
turquoise should be greyed,
slightly bluer and lighter. Again
there was difficulty in obtaining
blues of an exact sequence but
in a scale of gradations it should
be, with practice, easy to see if
one is out of alignment, as
shown.
    It should be possible to judge
too where a colour comes on a
grey scale, whether it is lighter
or darker than another colour.
This is valuable in translating
into tones from colours. Yellow,
the most brilliant colour, comes
near the light end of the scale,
while violet is over midway
towards the dark end, as it is
the least brilliant colour. The
other colours, when pure, work
upwards to violet–orange, red,
blue – each a little higher on
the grey scale towards black.

right
A panel by Kay Cosserat
worked on a navy rayon fabric,
entirely in loop stitch. The
interest is obtained by the
mixture of colours, in each
stripe merging from two to one.
The density of stitches makes
the colour brighter where the
background is concealed.
Sparsely scattered stitches are
duller with tones near to that of
the ground tending to merge;
the lighter ones particularly the
light green appears to stand out
Photograph by John Hunnex

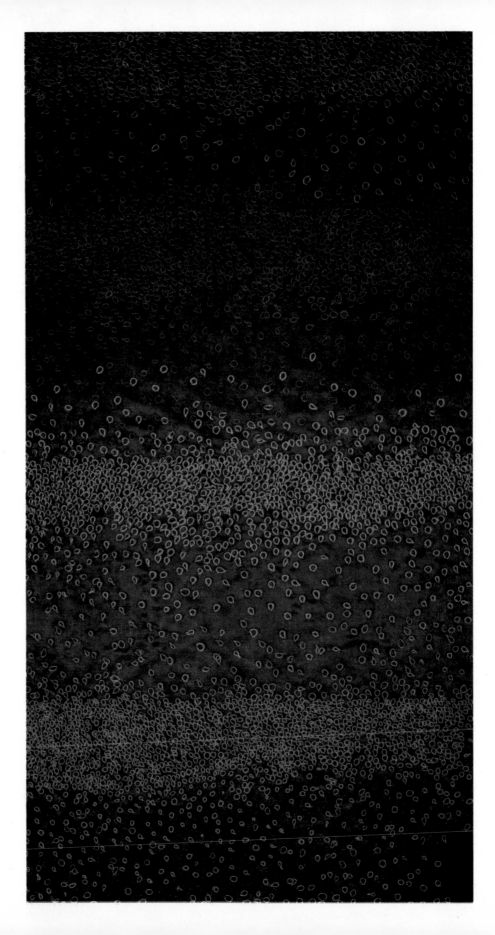

shapes being kept in place with small running stitches worked through the two sheers. Machine stitching can be used for outlining but gives a harder line to the shapes. Italian quilting in which narrow channels are stitched by hand or with the twin needle by machine, are threaded with brightly coloured wools, which show under a transparent fabric as delicate or sombre. Two layers of fabric are again used for this form of decoration, both transparent or the upper one only transparent.

This leads on to the use of padding and quilting where tones rather than colours are important. Italian quilting using opaque materials, where the channels are threaded with white quilting wool giving a raised, linear effect, is purely decorative and depends on the shadows of the channels for interest. In English quilting a complete design is padded, with the filling between two layers of fabric. The tones occur between the closely stitched areas which become flatter and those without stitching which puff up, creating darker and lighter areas according to the varied depths of the quilting. Padding may stuff complete, three-dimensional objects, semi-relief embroideries or small, isolated shapes in a design, such as is seen in trapunto quilting. This involves two layers of fabric, the under one being slit where the design is to be padded. With the small, raised shapes, surface embroidery in self colour gives an added richness of texture to the design. In fact, padded work which relies for its interest on light and shade has a quality which can be ruined if colour is added to it.

Other means of creating shadows and tones are by

Italian quilting on a large scale. The panel by Elizabeth Gault is 76 cm × 99 cm (30 in. × 39 in.), the ridges about 1 cm ($\frac{1}{2}$ in.) wide. The quilting is in white fabric in contrast to that of the darker, handwoven fabric which is dyed in subtle colours of greys, pinkish and greenish colours, all low toned. The result is dramatic in its simplicity of dark and light, raised and flat areas
Photograph by John Hunnex

pleating, gathering, ruching and tucking in a variety of ways. Gathering can bunch up materials in different directions and in different depths, creating very dark shadows, pleating or folding can conceal parts of patterned fabrics such as a checked gingham, where one of the colours can be partially hidden, or stripes can be folded to conceal one of two colours in a two coloured fabric. Tucks can be very small, creating narrow lines of shadow; or very deep and bent backwards, slit in parts, with the edges turned in to make patterns, stuffed as tubes or pressed to fold in particular directions. Irregular shadows are created by these means but interest may be emphasised with embroidery, as in smocking where the gathered folds are caught together with backstitch, but at random to give varied hollows and depths of shadow.

OVERLEAF *left*
Bedspread 2.6 m × 2.9 m (8 ft 6 in. × 9 ft 6 in.) by Nancy Britton, Massachusetts, USA Cotton and polyester blend broadcloth. The use of applied, gradated colours gives the appearance of transparent fabrics, although they are all opaque. The designer mentioned the fact that the colour print was paler than the actual quilt and also it did not blend so smoothly as in the original work, particularly in the dark red parts. Illusions of transparency using opaque fabrics and stitchery are fascinating colour exercises to try, with gradated colours or with colours of equal tones and their mixtures
Photograph by Boris Studios, Boston, Massachusetts

right
Panel 42 cm × 54 cm ($16\frac{3}{4}$ in. × $21\frac{1}{2}$ in.) by Kay Cosserat
In tapestry and crewel wools on a blue woollen background which is couched entirely in grey blue threads tied down with blocks of slanting stitches in various blues, with touches of pink, green and yellow. The centre panel is worked vertically and horizontally in groups of close stem stitch giving the feeling of threaded fabrics. The concentration of warmer light colours, merging into blues and cooler pinks and blues, the divisions between the stitch directions all help to give a raised, three-dimensional appearance. The surrounding border in blocks of chain stitch vary according to the direction in which they are worked and are mainly in one colour, with an occasional insert of yellow-green
Photograph by John Hunnex

Italian quilting with two layers of white organdie worked in running stitch by Jane Iles.
The left pattern is threaded with black wool, the centre one in grey, the right one in white, giving three distinct tones to similar patterns
Photograph by John Hunnex

Head – a sample for the doll by Jane Iles
In similar colours but with hair in various colours of wool. In both cases the eyes glare forth in bright blue thread
Photograph by Jane Iles

Padded doll by Jane Iles
A relief embroidery of a baby
doll in dyed stretch fabric of
pale pink. The background
consists of multicoloured but
delicate-toned flowers. The
shadows, which help to bring
the relief into stronger contrast,
are in fine seeding stitches in
browns. Here relief and tonal
variation give interest rather
than varied colour
Photograph by Jane Iles

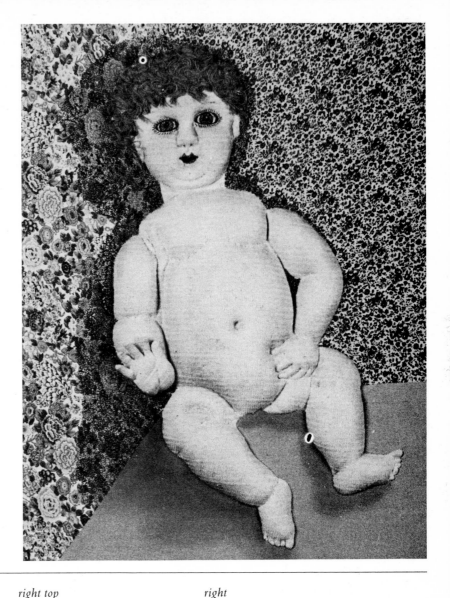

OVERLEAF *left*
Examples by Francis Challis of
colour combinations, in threads
wound on to strips of card
about 30 cm (12 in.) high.
Different proportions of stripes
and arrangements of colour can
be seen easily in this way. The
more pleasing ones can be
picked out from the collection.
The photographs shows the
stripes on a black background
and on a white background.
Some of them appear duller,
some brighter on the different
backgrounds
Photograph by John Hunnex

right top
Sample of canvas work by
Helen Wilshaw showing tints,
pure colours and shades. The
larger triangles tend to more
equality of tonal value than the
central small triangles which
are strongly contrasting and
together they appear to come
forward to make one large
triangle on a background of
larger, greyed ones
Photograph by John Hunnex

right
Stripes made over card by
Valerie Mosley using patterned
fabrics and coloured threads
This idea can be useful if trying
fabrics with threads, to see how
the colours work together, also
the ratio of patterned to plain
areas. If fabrics and threads go
together then they should be
suitable for a design but it
should be remembered that
stitches can change the colour
by their textures and the
direction in which they are
worked and patterned with
plain fabrics have more impact
than plain ones alone
Photograph by John Hunnex

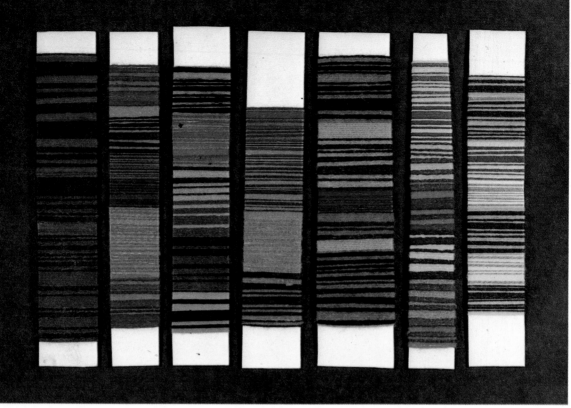

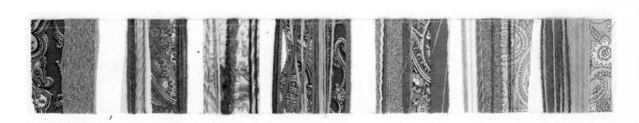

'Sun Bowl' by Phyllis Dukes, California, USA. A three dimensional form, stitched by machine with quilted areas and padding in different depths in fabric which has been tie-dyed to give a mottled effect. Colours are bright red, pink and yellow, the whole effect is full of vitality with shadows and variety in values of colour   38 cm (15 in.) diameter

'Recluse' by Phyllis Dukes, California, USA. A three dimensional, freely worked embroidered structure in appliqué of dyed fabrics in rust, navy and red. The loosely stitched fabrics give shadows and the raw edges impart a quality which would be lost if they were neatly turned in and hemmed. Stab stitching and running are used both to hold the structure together and to add interest to the plain fabrics about 28 cm × 25 cm × 15 cm (11 in. × 10 in. × 6 in.)

OVERLEAF *left*
Panel 42 cm × 66 cm (16½ in. × 28 in.) by Elizabeth Gault
Dyed yellow fleece on canvas. The sky is of hand dyed and hand woven fabric. The fleece is more thinly spread towards the top of the canvas, the base is thicker giving a quilted appearance. The apparent changes in the colour of the fleece are due to very close to open stitching in stab stitch and seeding in a variety of colours; red, blues, greens and pinks to whites, the closer the stitching the greater the colour change
Photograph by John Hunnex

right
Landscape by Susan Armitt
A very fine stranded silk is worked in herringbone, cretan and other stitches, one over the other giving a luminous quality. The variation in the colours of the threads gives depth. They tend to be in delicate tints or greyed colours. The grassy field is achieved by fraying out the extra length of fabric and turning it back on itself. The frayed threads are secured with machine stitching. The brilliant turquoise of the building shows up against the yellower green of the grass. Other colours merge to give subdued tones
Photograph by Ione Dorrington

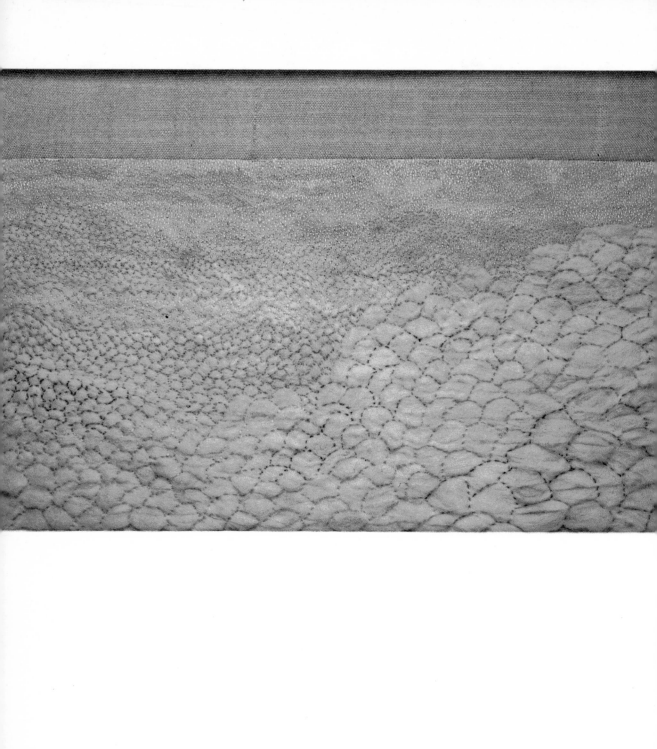

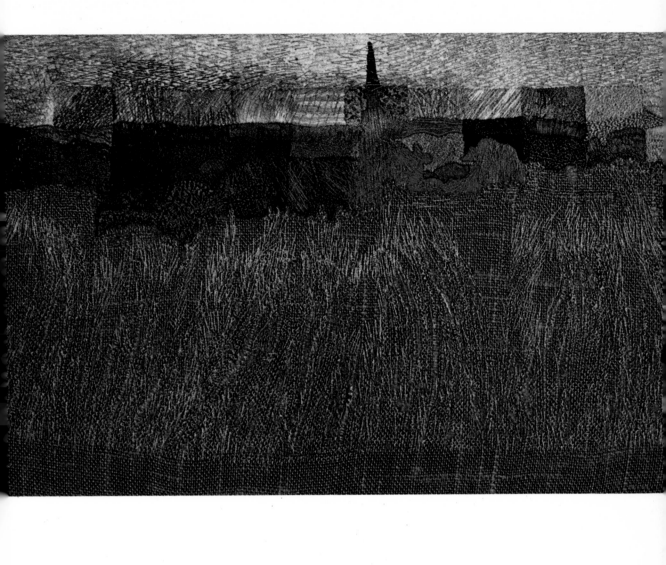

opposite top
'The Birds have Nests' designed
by Doris Hoover. A detail of a
three dimensional structure in a
number of fabrics, mainly
upholstery with acrylic and
wool threads.

The coarse and rough textures,
the depth of the bowl like
shapes which make shadows,
with fraying, broken edges,
with the thick, wrapped 'twigs',
altogether give a lively piece of
work
Photograph by Marion Ferri,
California, USA

opposite bottom
Detail of 'oriole's nest' by
Doris Hoover, California, USA,
in wrapped and stitched threads,
in dark to pale tones. There is
no wire in the structure, but the
three dimensional, cage like
effect is made more exciting
with the varied spaces between
the 'cage' ribs. The ends of the
wrapped threads are interesting
and are left loose deliberately
Photograph by Marion Ferri

above
Padded, detached feather shapes
by Susan Stone, lined and
overlapping to give slight
shadows. The background and
the shapes are covered in mole
coloured chiffon. Cream crêpe
appliqué is stitched by machine
in cream thread, the pattern
lines also are in zigzag stitching
in the same colour. The darker
lines in the background and the
narrow zigzag lines are light
red. Shadow work, herringbone
and cretan stitches in grey
stranded cotton emphasise the
slightly padded shapes. The
cream areas show up strongly
against the mole colour and
tend to jump out
Photograph by John Hunnex

95

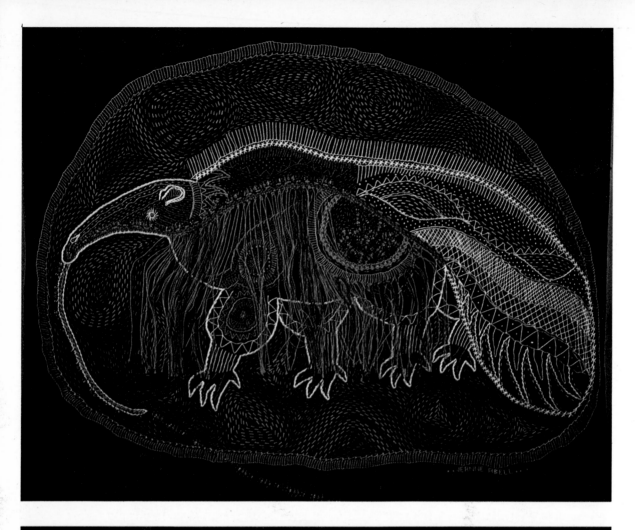

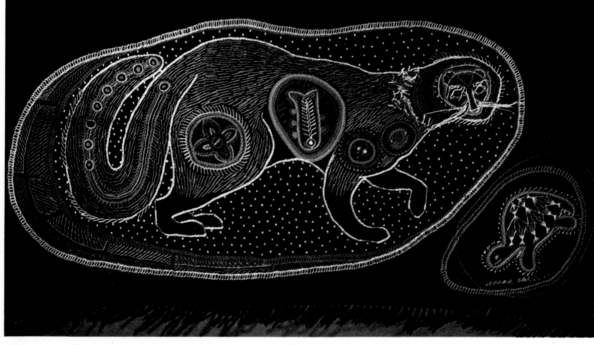

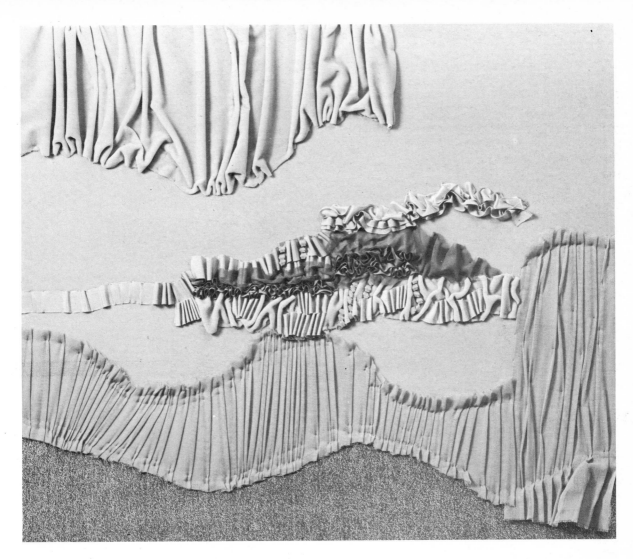

opposite top
'Anteater' by Jeanne Abell in white, greys and bright colours on a dark ground which gives added brilliance to the embroidery. The mainly neutral tones enhance the colours
Photograph by Richard Abell

opposite bottom
'Snow beast' by Jeanne Abell in browns, greys and white on a dark ground. Here the textures create interest and variety
Photograph by Richard Abell

'Landscape' by Pamela Whatmore
Folding and gathering of fabrics create tonal contrasts which give interest to neutral colours. The colour scheme is derived from the study of mushrooms. The background is beige velvet without a definite pile, the same fabric being folded at the top of the work. Darker velvet with a pink, slightly mottled in grey brown and beige makes the base of the embroidery over which darker beige chiffon is pleated In the centre a collection of fabrics is manipulated by folding, with uneven pleating and ruching, and includes background velvet, pinkish fawn and fawn grosgrain ribbons. The darkest part consists of straight cotton bindings, mingled with the velvet and ribbon
76 cm × 60 cm (30 in. × 24 in.)
Photograph by John Hunnex

opposite
Details – 'Study in light and shadow' by Doris Hoover, which describes this work exactly. The shadows and the dark fabric create contrast, the tucks and covered buttons give depth, with seaming making interesting shapes. Fabrics of linen add texture
Owned by Mrs Everett Berg
Photographs by Howard Fisher, California, USA

Calico gathered on the machine, by Susan Moss, to give a raised effect, also one of contrasting areas of textures, flat, ruched and puffed. Strong shadows give impact and depth to a fabric which is normally of ordinary texture and off white in colour. The results show interesting possibilities in creating lively textures with a plain, cheap fabric
Photograph by John Hunnex

Patchwork

Patchwork, which may or may not require stitches to complete the effect, is an excellent means of designing in tones, either with plain fabrics, patterned fabrics or patterned with plain ones. The interest is created by the choice and distribution of colours which should possess good tonal variations. Designs using patchwork can give intriguing illusions of depth, simulated with three or four tones correctly distributed. Padded areas to give real depth can be mingled with those which are really flat. The box patchwork already mentioned on page 33 is a simple example of apparent depth using three tones. The diagrams show a number of ways in which complicated patterns may be built up. Try out some of these in three or four tones of black, white and greys, then substitute colours for the neutral ones, after which invent patterns. On a smaller scale, particularly if working on canvas, similar ideas of apparent depth are worked easily in satin stitches Here the direction of stitch can add a further interest to the effect.

Refer to the old log cabin patchwork for an interesting use of colour and tone. Sometimes one half of a square is worked on the diagonal in a dark colour combination, while the other half is light. By this distribution of tones, diagonal stripes are formed, often giving an illusion of transparency but created with squares set straight.

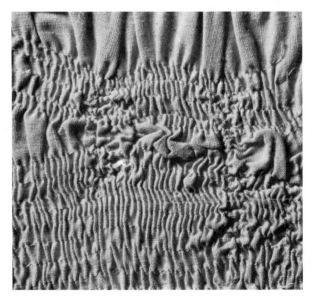

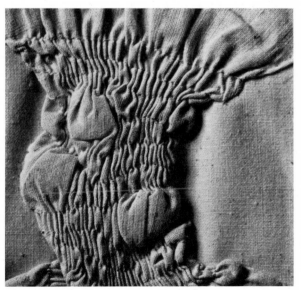

(a)

(b)

(c)

(d)

(e)

(f)

Patchwork is a means whereby the use of tones and colours, in plain and patterned fabrics, can create illusions of depth or of raised areas. If geometric patterns are worked out at first, freer, more complicated patchwork can be tried later as it is easy to get into a muddle. It is wiser to work out rough ideas on paper with the distribution of tones, than to make a collection of patches of random colours and tones that will not fit together. In all of these diagrams colours may be substituted for the greys, blacks and whites, but if to give a similar effect keep the tone values as in the illustrations.
(a) Could be carried out in two colours and white or in three tones of one colour
(b) Could be in three different colours for each of the two squares which could be repeated in any suitable sequence. For example a square could be in olive green – dark, cold pale pink light, with greyish yellow – medium; or it could be in navy, ochre and white. Try colours out before a decision is made on the embroidery
(c) Five tones have been used for this pattern which appears to come forward. Five tones of one colour would give this same effect
(d) A flat pattern in which any three tones could be used
(e) The same square arrangement as in (b) with a separating shape, in four tones
(f) Five tones of colour give a more complex arrangement of squares. The mottled surface could be stitched or worked as a patterned fabric. The four squares together could be repeated as a unit. Again colourways should be tried out first of all if disappointment is to be avoided.

below
'The Swing' by Kelli Bennett aged 16, Justin F Kimball High School, Dallas, Texas USA Stuffed appliqué in pale pink, bluish mauves and maroon, with some black areas, give the white quilt-like padded area good contrast for the figure. The small broken rectangular shapes help to break up the large white area

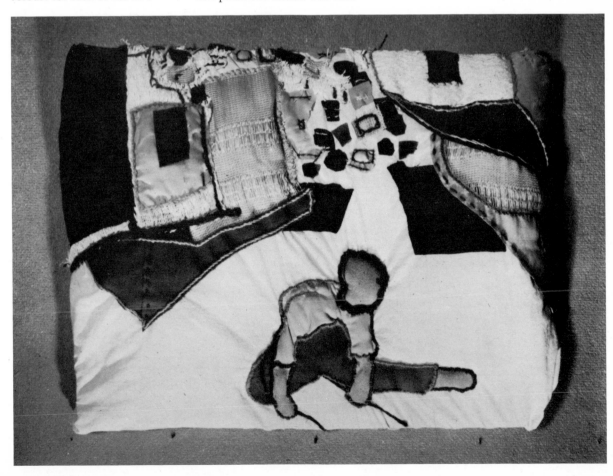

above and opposite
Details of 'Mesas' designed by
Doris Hoover. The contrasting
colours and textures of fabric
in wool, linen, velveteen and
denim; the use of various
widths of tuck, cording, machine
and hand stitching piecing
(sewing fabrics together) all
tend to give this work an
exciting quality both of tone,
texture and colour
Photographs by Howard Fisher,
California, USA

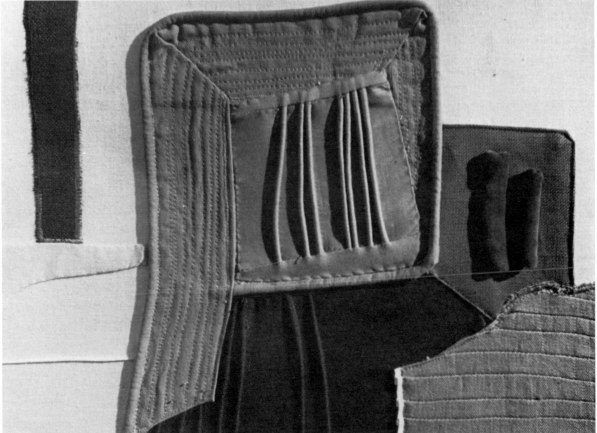

Patchwork patterns which show
suggestions for more intricate
designs. They can be repeated
over whole surfaces or used for
borders and isolated areas

'Landscape' by Linda Flower
Embroidered by hand on clear
plastic. It is not possible to
unpick this work as the plastic
would tear. The stitching is
worked spontaneously from
a pastel drawing of a landscape,
therefore it has a more painterly
quality than if a design had been
developed from the drawing.
It also has the vigour of a piece
of work enjoyed. The direction
of stitches echo the lines of the
drawing and are mainly long
straight stitches with knots,
couching and some stem stitch.
The brilliant colours bring the
foreground right forward but
there is good contrast of tones
in the greyer colours of the
background. The photograph
was taken with a grey, cloudy
background behind the plastic,
in order to emphasise the
colours
Photograph by John Hunnex

Fabrics

Very loosely woven, embroidered fabrics with cob-
webby textures look well hung with light behind them,
or they may depend on contrasting coloured backgrounds
which show through the laciness, giving depth to the
embroidery. Pulled and drawn thread work on scrim or
coarse hessian, evenly woven linens or muslin are in this
category; canvas with some areas only embroidered
showing light through the unworked parts where the
holes may be increased in size by pulling the open fabric
together makes successful hangings and screens, with the
fabrics placed behind the embroidery making them darker
or lighter, with larger meshes giving more contrast in tone.
Surface qualities of plastic fabrics vary, some being matt,
some shiny, while others are bumpy or textured like
leather, or are smooth like fine kid; they are opaque except
the clear white, transparent PVC which is unbacked; they
come in a wide range of bright or subtle colours, including
golds and silvers. For embroidery those backed with cloth
are best unless stitching directly onto the transparent
grounds. They may be worked as for leathers and suedes,
combined with woven fabrics, many of them taking
embroidery well, as they do not fray and are reasonably
pliable. Fabrics may be part dyed, 'scrunched' up or
crumpled in the hand, then painted, sprayed or spattered
with more dye before the embroidery is worked. When
these fabrics are smoothed out they will retain their original
colours in the unsprayed folds, the remaining areas having
mottled surfaces, which add an appearance of depth to
smooth surfaces. Other experiments will no doubt result
from these ideas and if they lead to more exciting embroidery and to further exploration of colour, they will
have been well worth the time spent in 'fiddling around'.

Simple counterchange in two colours or tones, which need not be strongly contrasting as in the black and white drawings. They could be quite near in tone, such as grey with white, violet with crimson. Where really subtle results are required counterchange of texture in one colour would make an interesting appliqué, such as using satin and wool, a patterned and a plain fabric, lace and chiffon. Many ideas will occur in which reversal of two fabrics has possibilities. The scale of a counterchange can be small or very large, such as in a banner or flag-like hanging, where simple contrasting shapes and colours are required

Use of stitches

Added to the many ways in which fabrics and dyes may be used, are the stitches which constitute embroidery, although collage and fabric manipulation are a basis of design in the beginning. The choice of fabric, its colour and texture take time. The selection of suitable threads and the translation of the idea into stitches which are expressive is often the most difficult part of the work. This is also the most important part as it is too easy to change the original concept of the idea completely with wrong choices. Stitches are a means of creating colour changes according to the direction in which the threads are worked. Exercises opposite demonstrate this. A stitch may appear darker or lighter than its true colour according to its direction. Worked spirally a stitch exploits all directions, and its tonal quality will vary with the source of light: satin, chain, stem, fishbone and basket stitches are good examples to try out as they show strong changes according to the ways in which they are worked. If the pattern twists and turns these stiches will appear sometimes lighter, sometimes darker. A shiny thread gives more positive results but fine threads such as crewel wool and the duller textures also change. The colour is affected by the closeness or openness in the placing of stitches next to one another and the amount of background visible. Herringbone, cretan, buttonhole and vandyke stitches vary in intensity of colour and texture according to the direction and the proximity of each stitch to the next. Raised stitches with rough surfaces tend to break up the colour with the shadows creating tonal differences. By combining both knotted stitches and smooth stitches into a solid mass of embroidery, using both dull and shiny threads in one colour only, the contrast of textures creates a richness comparable to working with several colours in one kind of stitch. As the background does not show at all, it can be of any colour in this instance. French knots, loops, raised chain band, bullion knots and similar stitches variously spaced and worked in colours of near intensity to that of the background, appear to alter its original colour where it is seen between the stitches. The closer these are, without becoming a solid mass, the more the colour of the fabric is affected. Red or blue or vice-versa, makes the blue look more purplish while a yellow green intensifies

Diagrams of stitch directions which show light and shade when worked at different angles. A shiny thread such as pure silk or perle gives the best results, but crewel wools and the duller cottons also give varied tones. Herringbone, basket stitch, fishbone and a number of canvas stitches show strong directional lines when worked

the blueness. A scarlet gives different results from using crimson, while a royal blue reacts differently from a greener blue. On a mid grey ground try working with colour of equal brightness. Where the stitches are closely spaced a cool colour makes the grey appear warmer, while red-orange stitches give a cooler look to the ground. Each exercise will produce changes according to those colours chosen, the spacing and the direction in which the stitches are worked and the textures of both fabric and thread, as a shiny surface reacts more than a dull one. Try some of these ideas out before reading about colour theory.

Raised stem band and padded satin stitch are smooth, and raised with less broken surfaces. Stitches repay experiment and when working an embroidery in mono-chrome or entirely in blacks or whites it is useful to know which stitches give tonal differences, the results in employ-ing all white threads or those of one colour only, being just as effective, sometimes more so, than when using colours where the beauty of a stitch may be overshadowed by strong hues. Stitches which show good variations in tone according to the way in which they are worked, i.e. closely, openly, upwards and downwards or in spirals are easily grouped, those good for lines being chain, stem, split stitches, and couching while among the broader stitches are basket, fishbone, leaf, cretan and satin. There are many others which should be tried out, also invented, as stitches are easily adaptable to colour experiments.

Freely placed lines, such as long running stitches, machine stitching, loose or couched lines in different weights of thread, if overlapped diagonally, can give a feeling of movement and create tone, using one colour only or several colours of thread. On transparent fabric they can be placed to be expressive on both sides where thick and thin lines of threads are worked closely or in open blocks so that where they lie on the surface of the fabric, the colours are stronger than when behind it. In several colours, carefully chosen, where the threads cross very closely, a depth of colour which scintillates is obtainable. Experiment with crossed lines in bright colours, in delicate or subtle colours, at different angles making some lines almost parallel, with some more diagonally placed. Work threads diagonally over patterns of narrow stripes and flickering movement will be obtained. Try one colour, then several colours over a two coloured, striped fabric

A detail of an embroidery by Mary Newland worked entirely in black thick wool thread on wool. This shows the light and shade obtained by using one colour but varying the stitch direction
Photograph by John Hunnex

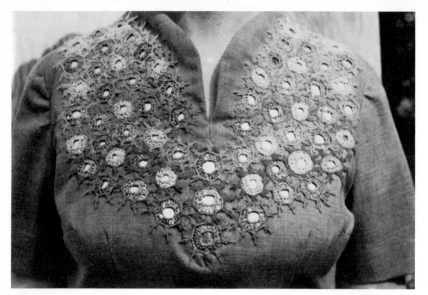

The yoke of a dress of lavender cloth, embroidered by Phyllis Hall, California USA, in reds, oranges and yellows with inserts of mirror glass. The result is rich with the concentration of very closely worked stitchery, merging from dark to light within a limited colour range

A necklace by Joanne Graham in needlepoint stitches (buttonhole) on a coarse scale. The richness is achieved with the near tones of colours in reds, oranges and pinks in solid stitching, with the insertion of small stones and lace fillings which contrast with the closely-worked circles. The changes in colour are subtle, merging almost imperceptibly

Panel by Valerie Mosley containing a screen printed plant form in black on white cotton, surrounded by a frame of long satin stitches in white stranded cotton.
The stitches show strong tonal variation according to the direction in which they are worked. The position of the light affects them, sometimes they appear as slightly raised, or the fabric appears to be raised. The whole panel is delicate in concept and, by change of position, the frame of satin stitches changes in tone
Photograph by John Hunnex

opposite
'Face' by Lynn Harris. On
green cloth, worked in grey
stranded cotton in buttonhole
stitches which appear to
change in colour according
to the closeness or openness in
their spacing and the amount
of background fabric showing
behind them. These stitches are
cleverly used to suggest the
solid form of the contour of the
face fading into the background
where the stitches are openly
worked
Photograph by John Hunnex

The interest is created by the
patches of dark and light and
the different widths of the stripes
worked in herringbone. The
illustration by Vivienne
Wolfenden shows an example
of the use of variegated thread,
in pale grey shading to black,
using a single thread of stranded
cotton. The embroidery is
worked on a greenish grey
furnishing fabric of medium
tone
Photograph by John Hunnex

'Pueblo' worked in buttonhole by Joan Schulze, California, USA This began as an exercise in using one stitch. The building was the starting point, in off white perle. The design, threads and colours evolved as the work developed. Transparent blue fabrics made the sky, and the whole idea became a colour problem, bringing shapes forward with dark purples and browns, with bright yellow stitching in the foreground 26 cm × 30 cm (10½ in. × 12 in.)

A sampler by Deborah Barclay worked entirely in french knots, in neutral tones of brownish grey, a lighter brown grey, cream, and a slightly greyed cream of equal tone value. The two lighter colours in the black and white photograph have merged, but results give a slightly transparent effect Photograph by John Hunnex

right
'Snow scene – Trees and snow crystals' by Helen Rumpel, New Mexico USA
White on white in a variety of threads some with thick slubs, some with very fine ones. The textures created by the stitches and threads make a rich embroidery with the depths of shadows giving a three-dimensional appearance. This work is effective in one colour as the textures are of major interest. Colours could have spoiled the unity

right
'Beach' by Helen Rumpel,
New Mexico USA
In very subtle tones of greys,
blacks, browns and whites with
various kinds of beads. Here
both the colours and the textures
complement one another. The
proportions of tones are good,
the foreground is light, very
textured, and becomes almost
three dimensional. Too much
similarity of surface is broken
by the mass of beads which give
a good point of interest, also
they add real depth to an
expressive piece of work

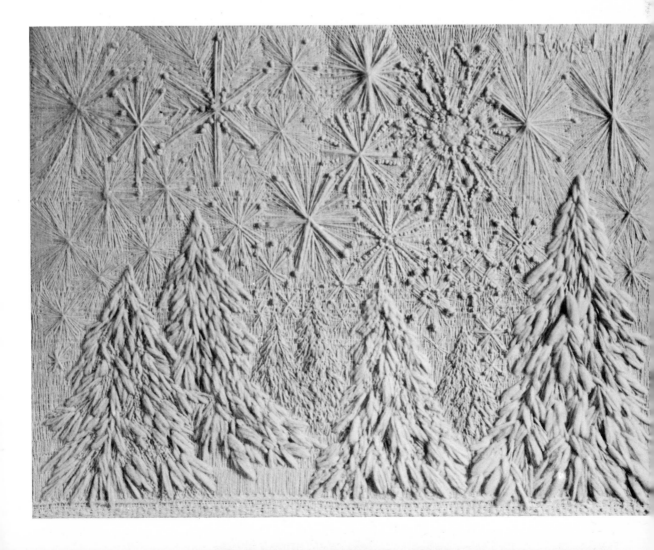

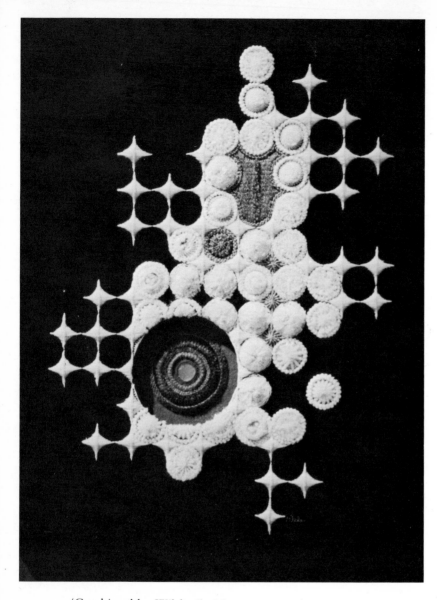

right, top and bottom
Two embroideries by Ksynia
Marko
The 'Tree' is in a hand tufted
stitch in greens, dull pinks and
yellow browns, on a gold linen
ground. Braid in gold metal
thread and burnt sienna silk is
applied and hand stitched over
parts of the pattern in yellow
green and the burnt sienna.
The 'Garden' is in similar
colours of hand tufting on a
grey ground; with white lace
appliqué and some white
stitching which appears strong
against the grey. The pale
patterns at the top are in tent
stitch and seeding in light greens
and yellow greens on a light
ochre ground. The tufting gives
strong shadows which contrast
with the flat stitching
Each embroidery 15 cm × 27 cm
(5 in. × 11 in.)
Photograph by John Hunnex

'Graphique' by Wilcke Smith,
New Mexico USA
A play on repeated forms with
four-point stars in padded
vandyke stitch. The large circle
exposes the back plane with
red and gold stitching
76 cm × 60 cm (30 in. × 24 in.)
Photograph by Bob Smith

'Face' by Lynn Harris. On cream flannel in ochre perle, showing changes of stitch direction and the way in which the colours are affected by the light as sometimes the stitches appear darker or paler than the actual colour of thread. Satin stitch and herringbone are used throughout this embroidery Photograph by John Hunnex

119

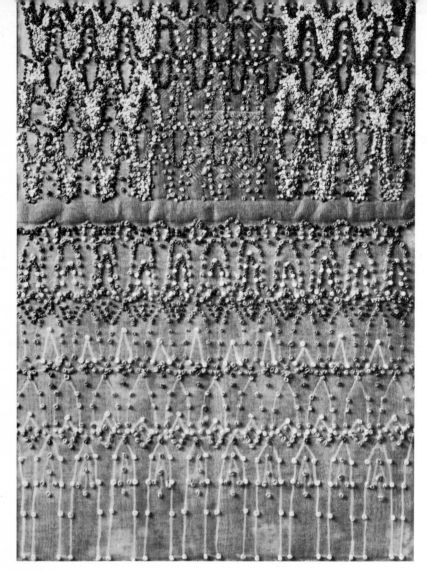

This embroidery by Paula Matthews has a background of brightly patterned cotton covered in white organdie. At the top is a fabric of brown and blue stripes, in the larger area below, scarlet and yellow flowers on an intense blue ground. The muslin reduces the strong colours to pastel tints, producing a charm and delicacy of background which is embroidered entirely in French knots, worked very closely to openly in greys, greeny greys and white threads. An interesting effect is obtained where the threads between the knots show behind the muslin and appear blurred like chalk lines. These are worked through the muslin only, others are worked through all layers of fabric

Photograph by John Hunnex

Shadow work

Shadow work is one way of obtaining delicate coloured embroidery using bright colours of thread. The stitches, either closed herringbone (double backstitch) and/or Indian shadow stitch are usually associated with this work and are sewn on the wrong side of a transparent or semi-transparent fabric. On the right side outlines in backstitch in the bright colours are seen round the shapes with pale, shadowy colours filling them, as the stitches on the wrong side cover the areas of the pattern behind. A more interesting way of working is to stitch on both sides of the fabric, to give bright outlines and patches of bright colour, with the pale areas. Other stitches are suitable for this embroidery

opposite
'Big Mamma' 81 cm × 58 cm (32 in. × 23 in.) by Marion Spanjerdt, Toronto, Canada Transparent and opaque fabrics are used for this embroidery in hand and machine stitching. The design is full of incident but the colours are limited – warm reds and yellows, cooler blue, mauve and some purple give unity to an exciting set of images. The large head in contrasting colours gives a good focal point, the merging heads in near tones, a good background

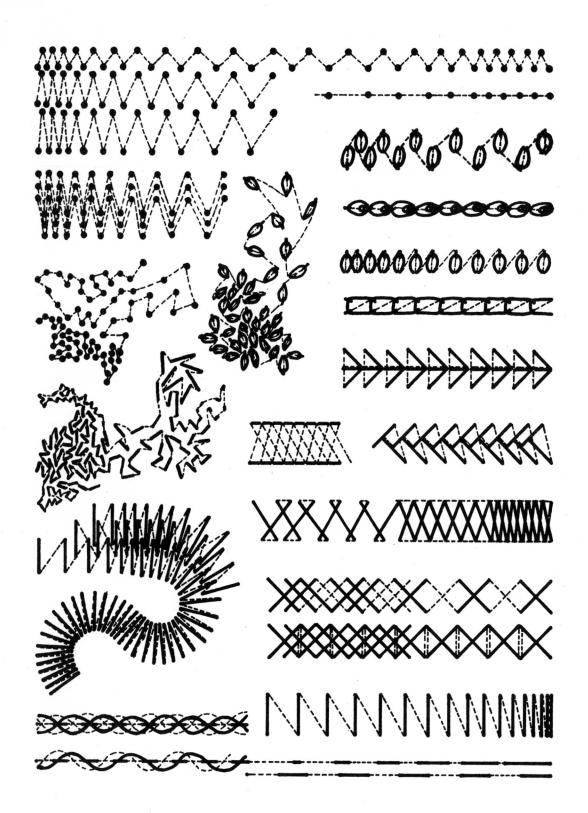

Diagrams of stitches worked on transparent fabrics. These show through from the back to the front, therefore give a different appearance from those worked on opaque fabrics. Hanging in front of a light – perhaps as a lampshade or a window curtain – the backs of the stitches will be particularly noticeable. The dotted lines in the diagrams indicate the backs of the stitches, the black lines those on the front of the fabric. With coloured threads on white organdie the stitches at the back appear paler, with black orandie they seem darker. With coloured sheer fabrics and coloured threads, preferably bright ones, the stitches behind will change in colour according to the fabrics into which they are worked. Straight stitches, chain stitches – detached – french knots, large seeding and running are some of the stitches suitable with the connecting threads joining the stitches making parts of the pattern

but try them out first. White on white, black on black, or light on dark and dark on light are all effective ways of decorating these sheer and semi-transparent fabrics with embroidery.

Blackwork

Blackwork is essentially a method of pattern making where contrast of tones is the main consideration. These patterns are worked on the counted thread of white linen in back and running stitches in fine thread such as one strand of stranded cotton, the tones varying with the open to closely worked patterns which are often emphasised in the darker areas with two or three strands of thread. In the reign of Henry VIII, colours, such as red or blue were sometimes worked instead of black, but were not mixed. The designs were emphasised with heavy outlines, often omitted now. Gold thread was combined frequently with the fine black silk, adding richness to the filigree quality inherent in the geometric pattern. Today other colours are used instead of white and black, but as the charm of the work is its laciness and delicacy, too many colours could destroy this and the subtlety of the tones which are a main feature of the embroidery.

OVERLEAF *left*
Part of an Indian hanging probably nineteenth century
The pattern is darned in fine, bright yellow silks, with a little pale turquoise, on a rusty red background. The direction in which the stiches lie gives noticeable light and shade to the colour, which appears to change considerably according to the source of light, and the way in which the embroidery is hung. The overall effect is of a very rich fabric
Photograph by John Hunnex

right
A knitted landscape by Becky Mullins
Gradations of colours, through blues and reds to yellows. Each stripe is slightly different in width. A band of stripes forming a diagonal strip is a focal point and is made by dropping the pattern of stripes below those of the background
Photograph by John Hunnex

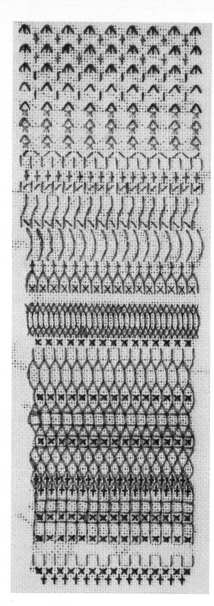

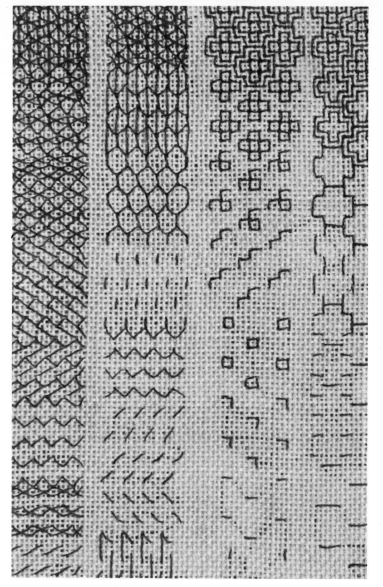

Counted thread samples by Lynn Harris based on black work. Tonal gradations are obtained by working open to close patterns, and by varying the thickness of the threads used, such as starting a pattern with a single thread, then doubling or trebling it until sufficient depth results.

The examples illustrated are *left* green and brown near tones, showing open and close patterns, using one or two strands of thread.

Above brown stranded cotton, one thread only, showing patterns built up from sparse stitches to many stitches, to give very light to darker areas Photograph by John Hunnex

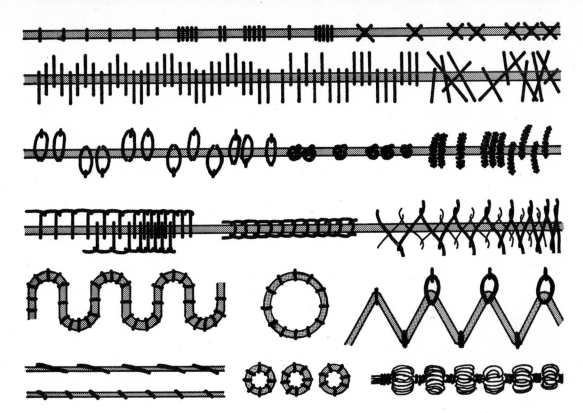

Diagrams showing ways in which threads may be couched down, to give a variety of textures. As couching means tying down one thread or set of threads with another thread or threads, a number of stitches are suitable for the couching down process. In the diagram, straight stitches, crosses, link chain, buttonhole, open chain and cretan stitches are shown. Thick threads may couch fine lines, dark ones tie down pale ones, shiny threads may couch dull ones down and vice versa. Several colours can be couched at one go, lumpy threads which will not go through material can be sewn down by couching. The bottom diagram (b) shows a complete skein of threads tied down with several stitches worked together at intervals. The skein is bunched up to give a series of blobs which are raised in contrast to the tightly tied parts. This effective decoration is seen on an embroidered garment from India together with satin stitch and open chain stitch patterns

Couching

Couching is a means of tying down one or more threads with other threads to follow a line in a design or, to make a solid filling, with a number of threads couched in lines side by side. Threads may be sewn down almost invisibly or in patterns, with similar or dissimilar colours and textures, the choice of thread dictating the result which may be smooth, or knobbly if being tied down, fine or coarse. Many colours may be put together in ordinary couching,

OVERLEAF *left*
Knitted landscape by Becky Mullins
A variety of manipulations of the fabric. The dark brown foreground is made stronger with the white of the background showing through the stitches, it comes forward in contrast to the three different greens which are bunched up but, with very little white showing through and look duller. The red fades to paler red and to orange at the top
Photograph by John Hunnex

right
A combination of knitting, dyeing and embroidery
51 cm × 64 cm (20 in. × 25 in.) by Becky Mullins. The foreground is strongly contrasting in part, the yellow greens leading up to the sun, which glows on the muted reds of the background. The light grey couched clouds stand out and appear to float

with a great diversity of effect. With roumanian and bokhara couching the thread being tied down and the tying down thread are one and the same, the difference being that the couching stitch is longer and diagonal and may be worked so that it scarcely shows in *roumanian couching*, while in *bokhara couching* the stitch is shorter and crosses at right angles over the thread making more defined stitches. With the diagonal stitches broad stripes of double threads and single threads give the appearance of lighter and darker areas of colour. Tonal contrasts vary according to the spaces between the couched threads, their thickness and texture, the background colour and the distance between the stitches which tie down the threads. Couching in which threads are tied down with different colours comprise endless experiment. Thick threads tied with thin ones or vice versa, using different colours and textures, such as black with white, yellow with pink; slub with smooth, shiny with dull, will in each case give variation in tone and colour, more noticeable if shiny and dull threads are used together. A thread may be tied down closely or with stitches far apart, with thin threads in pale

Embroidery designed by Susan Kearney. The embroidery has a cool, watery quality and is in light colours. Lime green repp is used for the background with appliqué in grey Thai silk and a small area of pale mauve velvet. The spaces set off the pattern which has a dynamic quality with its opposing rigid shapes and swirling couched lines, in a variety of textures and weights of thread. The negative areas are well planned, the richer textures emphasising the raised circle which is the focal point of the composition about 102 cm ⨯ 76 cm (40 in. × 30 in.)
Photograph by John Hunnex

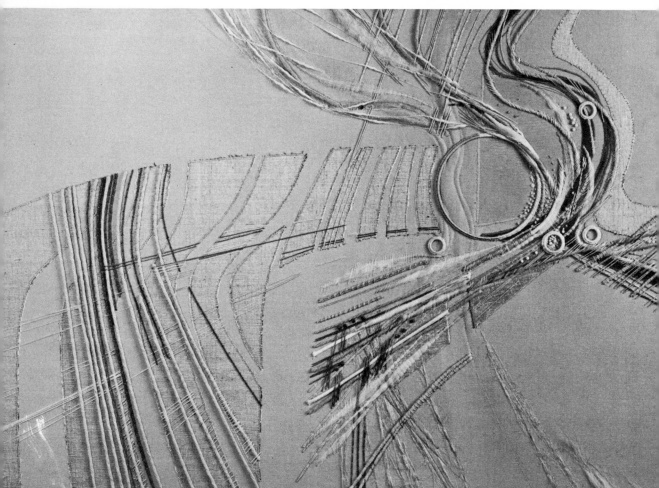

colours, varying to thick threads in dark colours; several threads of different or similar colours and textures may be sewn down with one contrasting colour or in a colour to merge with those being couched, or the thread may vary. For example red, white and blue threads could be couched into a broad band, with blocks of satin stitches in separate colours of red, white and blue to keep them in place, or alternatively blocks in one of the colours only such as all blue or all white threads could be used to couch down the three colours

---

OVERLEAF *left top*
'St George's castle plus one dragon' 38 cm × 37 cm (15 in. × 14½ in.) by Joan Schulze, California, USA
A free machine embroidery experiment in which the castle became very puffed up in spots. Some threads were removed and drawn work was put in for doors and windows. The white fabric was applied to an upholstery fabric ground in a very beautiful combination of reds, pinks, yellow and greenish near tones. Silk appliqué in blues, reds and yellows sometimes ruched up, with hand and machine stitching was added, the suggested dragon being indicated in machine embroidery

left bottom
'The Valkyrie', 76 cm × 50 cm (30 in. × 20 in.) by Richard Box
The sense of atmosphere is created by the colours and shapes of the flying figures. The sky recedes into the distance, in pale near tints of pinks and yellows, while the figures are dark and strongly contrasting. Machine and hand embroidery is combined with some padded areas
Photograph by Ione Dorrington

right top
'Acoma (Sky City)' by Joan Schulze, California, USA
Panel on a white nylon stocking over polyester filling stretched over a board. Transparent coloured fabric under the nylon stitched by hand, represents the sky. The pueblo acoma is hand stitched in six-strand floss, in yellows, orange, pale browns and reds; the red being in the foreground 30 cm × 40 cm (12 in. × 16 in.)

right bottom
'Portola Valley' by Joan Schulze, California, USA
A spontaneous work trying to obtain depth. Full, saturated colours in the foreground, greyed ones for the mountains. Appliqué over a nylon stocking stretched over a board, padded in parts with polyester filling to give a log-like effect. Fabrics in silk, knitted cotton, some in patterns of batik, with stitching 48 cm × 58 cm (19 in. × 23 in.)

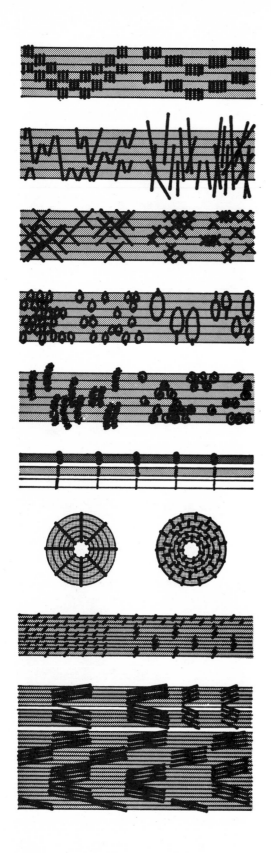

right
'Garden' by Rosalýnd Floyd.
The contrast in textures gives
vitality to the work. Machine
tufting in bright yellow green
perlé, mixed with finer pale
pink and green cotton, contrasts
with the flatter circles in whip-
stitch in two cool pinks with
bright and pale yellow and
yellow green thread. The flat
band is in bright green perlé in
chain stitch, the same colour
being worked as a rectangular
couched area. Dark bottle green
couching edges this shape and
fine bottle green threads are
mingled in the tufting. The
colours appear to change
according to the way in which
they are worked and the mixing
of colours together gives an
almost 'shot silk' effect in the
tufting
Photograph by John Hunnex

left
Examples of couching in more
solid blocks. The bottom, left
hand diagram shows roumanian
couching which is ideal for
making striped patterns in self
colour. This couching is worked
with one thread tied down
by itself in long, slanting
stitches. Where the double
thread occurs there is greater
weight in contrast to the single
thread, giving the effect of
stronger and weaker colour.
This method of couching is
particularly good used as a
filling stitch. Merging colours
look well couched down in
bands of solid stitching.
Working from dark to light
and back again a three-
dimensional effect is possible

OVERLEAF *left*
An example of shadow quilting
by Valerie Mosley in two layers
of white organdie, between
which are sandwiched brightly
coloured felts. These become
delicate and more subtle under
the white, transparent fabric.
Running stitches hold the shapes
in place, keeping the work alike
on both sides. Black organdie
substituted for white creates a
rich effect but is more difficult
to photograph
Photograph by John Hunnex

right
Two examples of pulled work
on linen scrim by Jane Iles
(a) Hand stitching showing
non-insistent, delicate colour
which adds charm to the
pattern
(b) Machine stitching showing
more variation in the depth of
the tones, consequently the
result has greater vitality
These embroideries show the
use of coloured backgrounds
with openwork patterns.
According to the depth of
colour, the work appears more
or less three dimensional
Photograph by John Hunnex

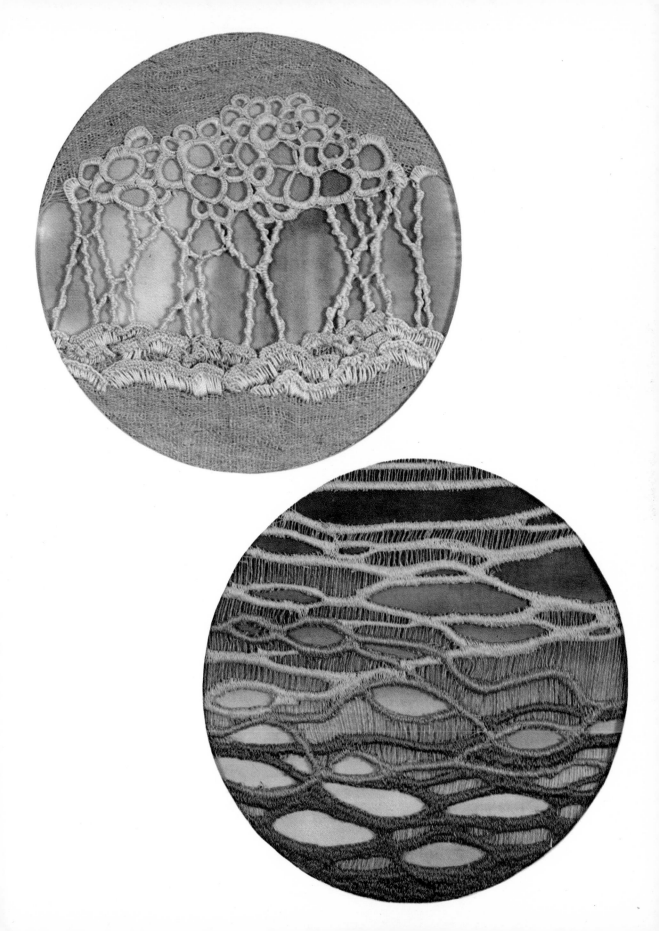

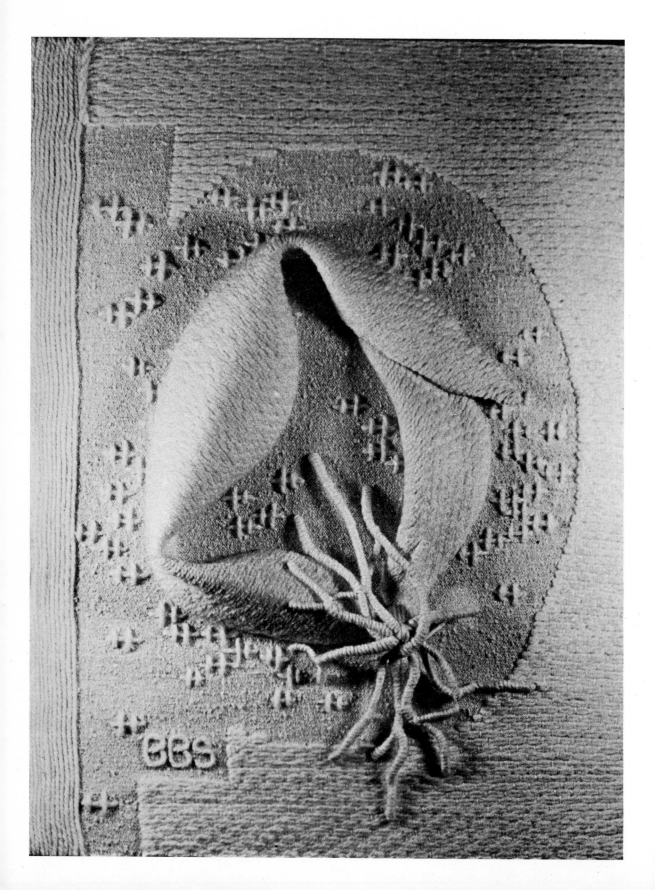

Part of a large hanging by Brygida B. Swiatowiec, Illinois, USA, on a background of white mixed cotton and rayon, mainly in couched threads, all in rug yarn. The entire work is in white and relies for interest on the textures of the Chinese cross stitch, the wrapped branches and the direction of working the couched threads. The shadows give a variety of tones. The draped area is covered in couched threads and is 8.9 cm (3½ in.) deep
61 cm × 76 cm (24 in. × 30 in.)

Laid work

Laid work is another form of couching in which shapes in a design are completely covered with fine threads, crewel wools or silk, or stranded cottons instead of silk; these threads by the direction in which they are laid show variation in both colour and tone. They are secured by couching threads laid over the shapes, in patterns, these being sewn carefully so that the laid threads do not part.

Metal thread embroidery

Different effects could be built up in a variety of ways; in some of the old Chinese metal thread embroidery, red, green and blue silks have been used to sew down gold and silver threads, giving an apparent change to the metal. With the reflections from the laid gold and silver threads the appearance is of more colour than has actually been employed, the results being rich and jewel like. Metal threads are fascinating to use and designs in which they are to be incorporated should be thought out carefully, as the great variety of tone obtained by reflection, from the direction in which the threads are laid, by tying down metal threads in coloured silks and by using different types of metal thread, otherwise can end in confusion. Jap gold worked solidly gives a smooth mirror-like surface; checks and purls break up the surface into facets of light and dark, while plate may be used smooth and flat or crinkled and raised. Sewn as invisibly as possible, with maltese silk, the metal predominates. By working in the old method of *or nué* or Italian shading, the ground is closely laid with

OVERLEAF *left*
'Chimayo apple dream'
47 cm × 37 cm (18¾ in. × 14¼ in.) by Bettie Ward-Johnston, New Mexico, USA
Light blue corduroy. French knots, stem, satin and back stitches worked in cotton threads. The foreground colours signify New Mexico earth. The white clouds are typical of the area, in which Chimayo is a small village, in N New Mexico, USA where there is great apple tree charm

right
Machine embroidery with a little hand stitching 18 cm × 23 cm (7 in. × 9 in.) by Rosalynd Floyd
The neutral greys give a brilliance to the stripe of clear blue, bringing it forward in front of the equally bright pink and yellow flower shapes. The spots of colour do not have the impact of the larger area of unbroken colour
Photograph by John Hunnex

gold threads with the pattern worked over them in coloured silks in burden stitch. In the past this method was used to increase the richness and brightness of the embroidery, with the gold threads glinting between the coloured silks, some stitches being worked very closely together, some far apart, to give a varied surface of gold. It is said to have been derived from enamelling in transparent colours laid over gold foil, which gave a jewel-like intensity and was practised on the continent during the fifteenth century. The effect changes according to the position in which the work is seen, sometimes the coloured silks predominate, sometimes the gold threads. Examples of this technique today are more widely interpreted and do not attempt to emulate those of the past. Couching down the metal thread with maltese silk first of all, then working over it with very little colour so that most of the embroidery gleams, partially or wholly concealing it in places, to give more solid areas of colour, contributes to rich but subtle results. Burden stitch, satin, fly stitch, herringbone, buttonhole and whip stitch are some of those which may be worked freely over metal threads to give broken or smooth effects, especially if the spacing of the stitches is varied. It would be wise to try out some ideas as samples before embarking on a large embroidery as the metal thread is costly and there are so many ways in which it may be used, besides the varieties in which it is made.

Running stitch

Running stitch is not only simple to work but also very effective and with it, broken and delicate colour changes may be made. The length and direction of stitch, the choice of threads and materials play a significant part in obtaining good results. On an opaque ground a thick thread can be worked to give the appearance of a spot or with a long upper stitch can look almost solid. On a transparent fabric with both the back and front of the stitch visible, although the back one is slightly fainter, a shimmering quality can be obtained with a number of rows worked together in fine, self-coloured thread. Delicate colour combinations are possible where bands of coloured running stitches cross over each other. If one or more colours of thread are employed, such as blue with red, where these cross an extra effect of transparency on transparent fabrics results

'Forest rain' by Ann Spence
Worked in bokhara and
Roumanian couching in perle,
stranded cotton and silk sewing
threads, these stripes achieve a
shimmering effect. The
background is white cotton
overlaid with blue grey and
mauve silk organdie. The
stitches are in green, grey,
mauve and black. Applied
stripes of white cotton stretched
over card give depth to the
embroidery, especially when
placed next to the dark stripes,
with a strong contrast in tone.
All colours are muted
Photograph by John Hunnex

where the two colours merge to make one. Knowing this, intricate patterns can be developed with coloured running stitches in groups of strong, primary colours or in delicate or subtle colours.

On opaque fabric horizontal, evenly spaced stitches in parallel rows, create stripes in a vertical direction if sufficient rows are executed. An embroidery worked entirely in this way but changing the colours from light to dark perhaps, or bright to dull, in stripes becoming progressively wider as the colours change, would be effective, as would blocks of colours alternating a sufficient number of rows of running to give a checked pattern.

Lines of long, even running stitches, or of uneven lengths of stitch, in fine threads, closely spaced, produce good textures where the direction of working can be exploited. Parallel rows of running, unevenly spaced both in length of stitch and spacing of lines, using a variety of thicknesses of thread in one colour only, give broken textured surfaces. In several colours, related in tones, surfaces suitable for large or small areas could be effectively stitched.

Whipped running stitches give slightly rough, wavy lines, worked close together in rows creating interesting surfaces, especially if two colours of thread or two textures are put together when a mottled result is achieved.

In a contrasting colour of thread, small, irregular running stitches worked vertically or horizontally over a background, to leave the pattern in the plain fabric and unstitched, can be effective. With a suitable design the stitches could follow the shapes, gradually filling up the ground, at the same time creating varied tones by their direction. Another effective means of texturing a complete fabric is to work with longer, more regular stitches over the background, using a self coloured thread but to change the colour over the pattern to a contrasting one, and to make smaller stitches, the direction in which the stitches could be worked depending on the intricacy of the shapes. All stitches could lie in one direction or the ground could be worked vertically, the pattern horizontally. To add variety to this idea, the weight of threads could be altered with a finer one for the background or the pattern, the colours could be reversed so that the pattern would be in self colour, the ground in contrasting colour.

Running stitches on transparent fabrics. Black thread on white or white on black, in perle no. 3, soft cotton, or coton-à-broder number 6, show grey through the fabric and are quite definite on the front. Primary colours look well on these fabrics. On coloured sheers, bright, thick threads such as perlé no. 3 or soft cotton look delicate from behind the fabric and change according to the colour on which they are worked, while on the front of the fabric they are bold. Running stitches are suitable for any articles which have to be seen from either side, such as blinds, stoles, scarves or lampshades

'Seascape' by Christine O'Connell. On a background of black cotton, the lines in backstitch, range from white and greys to several pinks, two tones of mauve and a bluish green. Very fine silver thread photographed as unbroken lines, intersperse the colours. The upright thin lines give an appearance of vertical areas, slightly greyed with the black showing through the spaces; while the area of horizontal, uneven widths of solid stripes appear to come forward on a different plane where their closeness gives concentrated colour. Solid buttonhole stitch in mauves with very closely backstitched shapes in between, show no background. The colours look much brighter against the black but as they are light to medium, the black background shapes outlined in dark grey seem to come forward

Photograph by John Hunnex

left
Running stitches although
comparatively simple to work
are very effective. The diagrams
show irregular stitches, regular
ones, long ones, short ones,
closely worked or far apart,
crossing over one another to
make patterns. On transparent
fabrics in one or more colours
of thread they look effective in
parallel rows worked closely in
wide bands. The backs of the
stitches will show as paler
colours through these fabrics.
Self coloured threads combining
thicker and thinner ones,
worked in running stitches in
parallel rows whether on
opaque or sheer fabrics, give
good textural areas. If several
colours are used, they may be
arranged to make definite
patterns

above
'Bird'. The background of the
bird is screen printed on hessian
in a rust dye, leaving its shape
in the colour of the fabric.
Copper waste is kept in place
with long copper coloured
glass beads. Running stitches
are in rust threads. The contrast
in tone is obtained with the
open stitching and the closer
placing of the beads which
shine on the copper and cast
slight shadows. This bird was
printed and worked by two
six year old girls, Jane
Czerswinki and Melanie Smith
Lent by Cathy Brooks, Holtspur
County First School,
Beaconsfield, Bucks.
Photograph by John Hunnex

Darning

As the threads must integrate with those of the fabric, they should be chosen of a similar thickness to that of the weave. Try out colours and stitch lengths and make sketches of the distribution of the pattern and colour to show the direction in which the darning is to be worked.

Pattern darning is really a development of running stitch and again varying tones of one colour can be created by the direction of the darning, the picked up threads of the fabric make the pattern lines, the direction in which the stitches are worked gives the tones, whether the threads are shiny or matt or of more than one colour.

Damask darning in which both sides of the pattern are alike is a fascinating means of exploiting colour as the darning is worked both vertically and horizontally to give this result. Working in two colours of thread, one in each direction, or in two tones, a result similar to that of shot silk is possible.

Double darning with stitches and spaces of equal lengths, as the spaces are filled on the return journey, is a good way in which to use many colours, particularly in geometric patterns of stripes, checks, chevrons and other regular shapes. This darning on fine, semi-transparent fabric in self-coloured threads is attractive and looks slightly raised. It shows a broken tonal quality. Plan patterns for darning on squared paper for greater intricacy. Darning the background of a design, working in different directions but leaving the pattern in silhouette may be carried out in one or more colours or in tones of a colour.

Japanese darning is open, consisting of horizontal and diagonal stitches. It has a lacy quality and worked in two colours on a transparent fabric looks very delicate. Variation is obtained by changing the scale of the stitches and by reversing the position of the two colours from horizontal to vertical and vice versa. The backs of the stitches give a shadowy effect to the pattern on sheer fabric, the effect on an opaque fabric is quite different. White thread on fine white fabric, or pale tints on the white give a shimmering look to a design.

An embroidery by Amanda Levy based on figure drawings, in tints of pale greys and pinks, on a pale pink linen ground. The central area is a network of straight stitches pulled through the fabric, the surrounding, outer areas are in satin stitches, darning and cross stitches, worked on the counted thread of the material. Darning patterns make blocks of colour in the hair. Stem stitch and running stitches emphasise the outlines in darker pinks and greys. The feature of the embroidery is its rich textural quality, rather than the colour, which, had this dominated would have spoiled its particular qualities   51 cm (20 in.) square
Photograph by John Hunnex

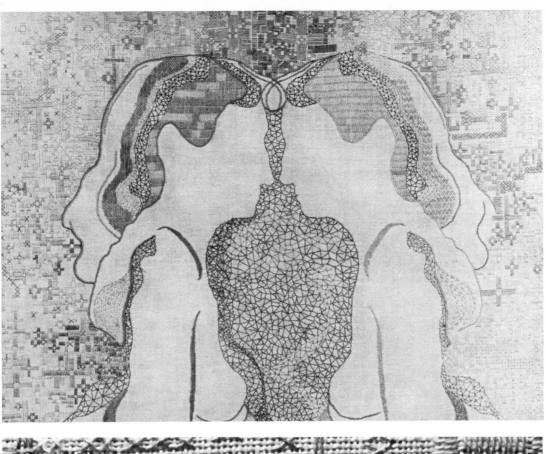

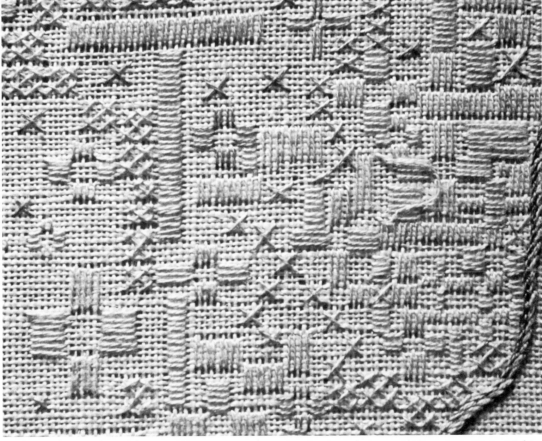

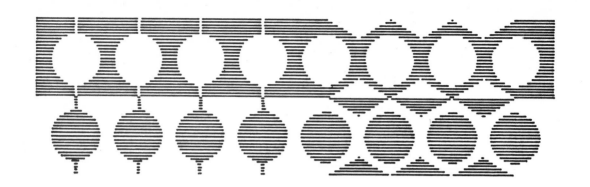

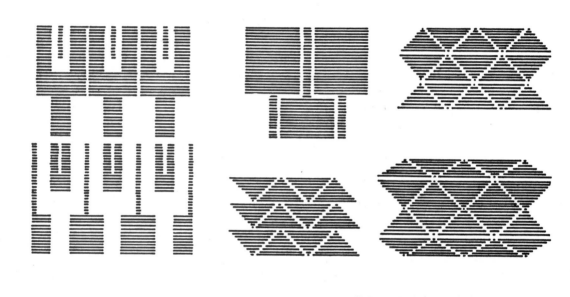

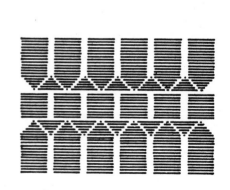

opposite
Patterns suitable for darning.
The reverse sides of these
are interesting and stripes in
alternate patterns could be
worked in different colour
arrangements. Gradated colours,
with threads ranging from light
to dark, or the reverse, would
work well in the small,
triangular shapes. Variegated
threads would give interesting
colour distribution in any of
these patterns.

Regular darning should be
carried out on fabrics with
easily counted threads, with
warp and weft of equal weight.
The working thread should be
as near as possible in weight to
that of the fabric

To exploit darning in colour

(a) Work examples of damask darning on a white ground
to show the use of

two tones of one colour

complementary colours

analogous colours

grey and white on a coloured ground

white or black on the opposite coloured ground.

(b) Work a small design containing areas of solid pattern
darning, lines of back stitch and Japanese darning. Use any
number of colours on a darkish ground such as navy or
dark red.

(c) The same pattern could be worked in white on white.
Coton-à-broder in a thickness to suit the fabric is a suitable
thread in which to work these patterns.

An excellent example of darning is seen in the Indian
hanging, illustrated on page 125, where a deep yellow silk
is darned in patterns on a rusty reddish brown cotton.
Occasionally a little brilliant turquoise blue silk is introduced among the yellow patterns, looking almost jewel
like.

below
Darning in two different
directions, using two colours of
thread. Intricate patterns may
be built up by this means, both
sides of the fabric being visible,
or only one, according to the
design and the purpose for
which the finished work is
intended. With vertical threads
in one colour and horizontal
ones in another, a shot silk
effect is possible

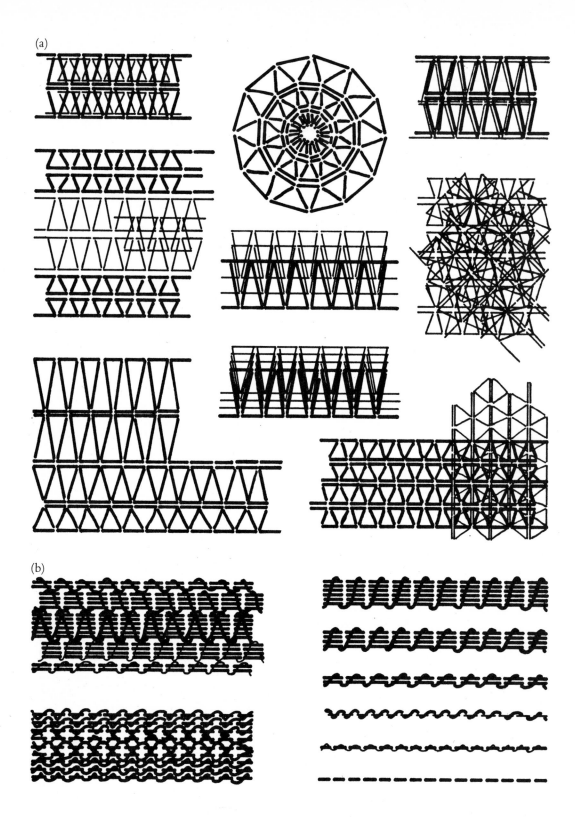

(a)

(b)

(a) Japanese darning is not widely known. It consists of two stitches to complete the pattern, a horizontal and a diagonal one and two colours may be used to make an effective area of stitching. The stitch may be made larger or smaller and fine or coarse threads employed according to the scale required. On sheer fabrics, a delicate, lace like result can be obtained with this stitch. Double rows of stitching in two weights of thread are effective and in colour can produce an appearance of shadows. Other ideas can be developed from the diagrams and by experiment

(b) Whipped running is effective on opaque fabric, worked in close rows. Long stitches whipped give a wavy texture. A thick thread such as soft cotton, tapestry wool or rug wool, are all effective. One colour or texture of thread whipped with an opposite colour or texture gives a mottled surface if rows are closely placed and combinations of textures and colours together can give many alternatives. Bands of running, whipped with other colours, as in the diagrams, are interesting to try out, the results depending very much on the weights of thread used and the version of the whipping.

Canvas work

Embroidery on canvas is an ideal way of exploiting colour as stitches can be merged imperceptibly from one colour to another, they can give clear-cut bold shapes, making definite statements; two colours of thread can be used in one needle to give a broken coloured surface, while a number of stitches and patterns are suitable for working in two colours. Some of these are more obvious such as rice stitch, smyrna cross stitch, reversed cross stitch and double stitch, where one stitch is composed of two put together, or two stitches make up the pattern. Merging stitches, provided that the tones of the threads are near, are florentine (sometimes called bargello or flame stitch), encroaching gobelin and long and short stitches. Examples of canvas work are seen on pages 156 to 159.

The canvas may be completely covered with stitches or parts may be left bare; freely worked stitches and those made by counting threads may be mingled.

To try out colour combinations

(a) Start with stitches requiring two separate movements, such as rice stitch. Work dark over light colour, bright over dull, then reverse the order. Work an area of stitches of one kind, changing the colours to make a definite pattern of colours and tones.

(b) Work in tones of one colour with merging stitches from light to dark and back to light ones again. With some experiment interesting three dimensional effects can be obtained in this way.

No doubt many other ideas will be thought of using specific colours and methods of work. An idea often suggests a colour scheme, or a purpose gives an indication of the kind of scheme most suitable for this purpose. Exciting colours, on the other hand, can foster ideas.

From the suggestions already given, the many ways in which colour may be exploited in embroidery could last a lifetime. The same colour worked in a variety of stitches, the same stitch worked in a variety of colours, apart from the many weights of thread available and the many fabrics and textures, although exciting, make it difficult to decide what aspects to emphasise in any embroidery. The more it is explored the more intriguing embroidery becomes. The emphasis of stitch direction, textural surface of stitches, manipulation of fabrics and different ways in which they behave, the use of transparent fabrics or dull versus shiny ones, have particular qualities which, if understood, mean also an understanding of embroidery as a creative medium in its own right, rather than being used to imitate line drawings or to carry out ideas better interpreted in other media.

Canvas work mask by Mieke Solari, California USA
Full size mask showing a subtle use of slightly greyed pinks and browns. The features are emphasised by brilliant orange and pink, bringing them forward against the duller ones. The beard is made of wrapped tassels, in wools in pinks, oranges and browns

'Spring' A cube 10 cm (4 in.) square by Jo Reimer, Oregon, USA in canvas embroidery. Varied textures of French knots, tent and other stitches in wool, cotton and linen threads are combined with shisha glass and resin blobs. The interesting textures create a rich, chunky piece of work. The colours in yellow greens, greens and yellows, with a little blue, suggest a delicate spring like scheme

left
Canvas work cushion by Mieke
Solari, California USA
In near tones of reds, slightly
greyed orange and tan, with a
cold discordant bluish pink.
Tufting, fringing and various
canvas stitches are combined in
a lively result. The back of the

cushion has applied fabrics in
dark and bright reds with
tufting and fringing as on the
front of the cushion. The
colours are mostly warm and
limited to those in the reddish
range

above
Embroidery on canvas by
Becky Mullins, parts of which
are left unstitched. Satin stitch
and long vertical stitches are
used. Colours are pale, tints and
greyed tones, with a darker rust
to add liveliness to the 'pastel'
scheme
Photograph by John Hunnex

Colour mixing

Practice in mixing colours in paint or other suitable media is necessary if designs for embroidery are to be worked out on paper for clients, or to show alternative ideas before a final decision is made on a design. One way to start is to try to match fabrics by mixing colours; then make them darker or lighter with the addition of black or white or with water. Make mixtures of colours, keeping notes at first on how these have been obtained. As skill increases, this will be unnecessary. Media such as water colour, poster colour, gouache, coloured inks, felt tipped pens, etc. are all suitable and may be supplemented by coloured papers.

It is useful to know which colours to mix together to obtain those nearest to the pure hues of the twelve segment colour cicle although coloured paper can be used. Watercolours, gouache, poster colours, etc. are suitable but the primary colours of red, blue and yellow do not give the gradations of colour needed for the circle. Those suggested in the following list, mixed in the right proportions (which result from practice) should be reasonably near in colour gradation.

Red which is neither vermilion nor crimson is nearer cadmium red.

Blue which is neither cobalt nor ultramarine, is nearer cerulean and when mixed with ultramarine makes a good clear blue, or cobalt mixed with ultramarine is satisfactory.

Yellow is between lemon and gamboge, a mixture of cadmium yellow with lemon yellow is satisfactory.

Orange – vermilion with chrome yellow or orange yellow is good.

Green – prussian blue with chrome yellow, or peacock blue and a mixture of chrome and gamboge give reasonable greens, but these must be tried out to see which one best suits the gradation of scale.

Violet – crimson and ultramarine give a clear colour, or cobalt violet used alone is satisfactory.

Blue-green – turquoise with a little ultramarine, or blue with a touch of lemon may be right in the scale. Again the mixture must be tried out.

Oil pastels and good wax crayons are brilliant if put down as strokes of pure colour on a white ground. Grey worked over the colours produces dullness. Other colours are a mixture of those already mentioned and practice in mixing pigments to match fabrics and threads will make it easier to put down colours when designing on paper. The diagrams show

1 The circle with twelve divisions of colour as pure hues. Those opposite each other with similar numbers or equal tones indicate complementary colours.

2 The circle with white on the outer edge to represent tints; mid grey, the pure hues and black in the centre, the shades. Every pure colour mixed with black becomes darker and a shade, while a pure colour mixed with white or is diluted to a paler colour becomes a tint. A pure colour mixed with black and white (grey) becomes a tone and duller. Between the black and the white, colour gradations may be very small, the more gradations the more circles of colours, until the pure colour becomes black, or white.

Colour
principles

An important point to remember is that no colour is seen in isolation, every colour is relative to those around it and is affected to a greater or lesser degree by them.

A brief account of colour and terms applied to colour are useful when reference is made to these in other parts of the book, but to see colour, observation is the best way by which colour behaviour is understood. For books giving deeper, more detailed study of its scientific properties see the bibliography.

Colour depends on light which is one kind of radiant energy made up of electro magnetic vibrations or wave lengths. The longest wave length is red, the shortest violet and they are between 400 and 700 millimicrons. The ultra violet rays are below 400 millimicrons and shorter with higher energy radiation, the infra red rays are above 700 millimicrons and longer with lower frequency and energy radiation. Light travels at an equal speed and carries energy, some of which is absorbed when it meets an organic substance. When the wave lengths between 400 and 700 millimicrons are seen equally by the eye, white light results, but if the wave lengths vary the colour changes immediately.

White light is composed of red, blue and green light. Pigments in which red, blue and green are mixed make dark grey or black, according to the proportions in which they are mixed. When light is mixed greater brightness results, but when pigments are mixed they result in duller, darker colours, unless white is added. The primaries of light are called additive as any colours can be made with red, blue and green light. Pigments absorb some light and reflect or subtract others and are called subtractive colours. For example – magenta absorbs green, therefore blue plus red = magenta. Turquoise absorbs red, therefore blue plus green = turquoise.

The rainbow colours are seen as a result of sunlight or white light passing through a prism, the light being bent or refracted and split up into this order, violet, indigo, blue, green, yellow, orange, red. A rainbow is seen in the sky when the atmosphere is wet with rain but the sun is shining on the curved raindrops which act as prisms and split up the sunlight.

No substance is coloured but the surface absorbs the rays which are not reflected in its colour. These surfaces are called selective surfaces. For example, a red object absorbs the green and blue light rays, resulting in red. A white surface is the result of a surface reflecting all colours equally but black is the result of absorbing all colours. The kind of surface affects the colour of an object, a rough or smooth surface reflecting differently, also the angle at which the light falls on the object, whether it is high or low and the intensity of light whether powerful or weak changes the quality of the colour. In a clear, smokeless atmosphere colour is more pure than in a sooty or foggy one, near to, it is much more intense than in the distance when it becomes greyer, and loses much of its purity.

Two people may stand very close together but their positions are not exactly the same, their eyes and their focussing powers are different, therefore they cannot see colours in the same way. Shadows move very quickly and light shifts constantly so that it is always changing as things are being observed. A colour described by one person is given a different description by another, blues and greens often causing confusion.

Matching fabrics is not easy as one seen in a bright light can change in a dull one; a shiny fabric on a dull day looks different in colour on a sunny day. Fabrics chosen in artificial light may appear quite changed in a natural light. This makes it important to select them according to whether they will be seen at night or during the day. Blues and greens appear more vivid in artificial light but many reds become dull and lifeless. This makes the choice of fabrics and threads difficult as if an embroidery is to be exhibited, artificial lighting can change its appearance from

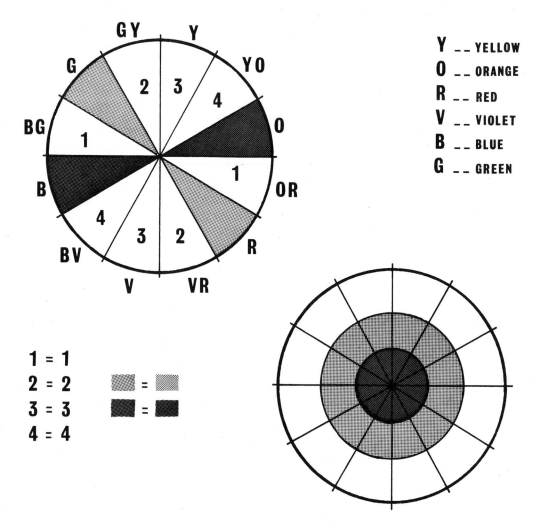

Y _ _ YELLOW
O _ _ ORANGE
R _ _ RED
V _ _ VIOLET
B _ _ BLUE
G _ _ GREEN

1 = 1
2 = 2
3 = 3
4 = 4

| B | B +1 | B +2 | B +3 | B +0 | 0 +3 | 0 +2 | 0 +1 | 0 |

This set of diagrams shows the names of colours in the colour circle. There are many books that display colour circles as reference if necessary, therefore in colour they have been omitted here. The lettered circle gives the gradations of colours in a twelve segment arrangement, from yellow, through orange and red to violet and back through blue and green to yellow. The numbers show the colours opposite each other, which are complementary, such as 1 is opposite 1 = blue green opposite

liveliness to drabness, causing much disappointment. Fabric samples in two or more colours can look quite different in the piece as from a distance some colours merge to create another colour. An example of this was to see a woollen fabric in narrow red and green stripes as a sample, where it appeared exciting. When this fabric was made up into a garment it became dull and brownish and lost its vitality as the two colours happened to be complementary to each other.

orange red. Mix these and they become a darkish grey or black. The three circles, one within the other, show tints round the outside circle, pure hues in the second circle and colours mixed with black in the centre circle. The finer the gradations from the pure to darker or lighter colours, the more numerous the circles, each one of which would contain colours of equal value. Most threads are obtainable in about five different tones; from bright to darker or lighter. Finer gradations, if required, must be made by dyeing white threads a sufficient number of times to obtain these gradations. Working with a scale of gradated colours can give a transparent effect.

The bottom diagram shows two opposite colours in the circle, at either end of a rectangle. By mixing each colour progressively, with a little more of the opposite colour, the results end up with pure colours mixed equally to give grey or black. In between, subtle variations of mixtures result. They may be obtained by dyeing too, but practice is needed in order to judge the quantities of each colour and the time needed for dyeing each of them to the required strength

A colour circle is included in this section as a guide to complementary colours and to analogous colours. Otherwise experiment is the only way in which to find out how to use colour. In the past many different colour circles were constructed, the first was made by Isaac Newton in 1676, where he used the colours of the rainbow. Chevreul in the nineteenth century did a great deal to add to the knowledge of colour behaviour but until recently red, blue and yellow were considered as primary colours which could not be mixed; however, Herbert Ives, an American, found that he could mix red with magenta and yellow, blue with magenta and turquoise but yellow remained as it was. Today red, blue, green and yellow are often thought of as primary colours. The secondary colours are orange made from yellow plus red; violet made from blue plus red; green blue made from green plus blue, and green from yellow and blue. Olive is made from green and violet, citron from green and orange, and russet from orange and violet. Tertiary colours are mixtures of secondary colours. A twelve segment colour circle is sufficient for explanation and for reference when colour terms are mentioned.

Terms

The main terms used in colour are

The hue The name of the colour, whether red, blue, yellow. Meaning its category or group as blue can be redder or greener but the blue predominates.

Intensity or chroma The purity or dullness of a colour. The purest is saturated colour – neither on the warm nor cool side but clear and unadulterated. The brighter the colour the higher the chroma, orange being high and pure while fawn and dullish pinks are greyed colours and low in chroma.

Value is the lightness or darkness of a colour – giving tints and shades in relation to black and white. Colours with black added become shades, with white added they become tints.

Tones are pure colours mixed with black and white, giving greyed colours according to the proportions in which they are mixed.

Chromatic colours Those originating from the mixing of pure colours, in different proportions.

Achromatic colours Those made from mixtures of black and white making neutral colours.

Complementary colours Colours of equal value, that is from one circle, opposite to each other. When mixed they make grey. However many divisions the circle has, the positions of the main colours and those in between remain constant, one colour being warm, the other cool. Large areas of complementary colour are scintillating; broken into small areas they become dull.

Split complementaries go together and are those on either side of a complementary colour. For example yellow is opposite violet, so that the split complementaries would be violet red and violet blue. In reverse, violet goes with yellow green and yellow orange.

Analogous colours adjoin each other in the colour circle, looking brighter together. The edges of these colours merge and the colours can appear almost as one from a distance. Broken into small areas the colours merge but are vibrant.

The after image concerns the fact that if a particular colour is concentrated upon for a few seconds on looking away from it at a plain white area, again after a few seconds the same shape appears but in the complementary colour. For example if the red ball of the setting sun in a pale greyish sky is stared at, on looking away a greenish sun will float before the eyes.

Simultaneous contrast is a result of the eye seeing simultaneously the complement of any given colour. This is a sensation in the eye of the observer, not present objectively. It is the basis of colour harmony and can be noticed by carrying out an exercise which is suggested by books on colour. Six squares, each 8–9 cm ($3\frac{1}{4}$–$3\frac{1}{2}$ in.), of the primary and secondary colours, have small grey squares about 1 cm ($\frac{1}{2}$ in.) in size and of an equal tone to that of the colour placed one in the middle of each colour. Each grey square becomes tinged with the complementary colour of that surrounding it, so that each appears slightly different, although they are known to be all the same colour. This simultaneous contrast also occurs between two colours not exactly complementary, each one pushing the other nearer to its own complement, so that each loses part of its contrasting colour. Every colour is affected by that next to it, to a greater or lesser degree and mid-grey reacts quite strongly. For example, a cotton dress fabric in stripes about 6 mm ($\frac{1}{4}$ in.) wide in scarlet and mid-grey appeared to have bright green edges after looking at the fabric for a few seconds.

Other contrasting colour combinations possess definite qualities such as (a) contrasting hues, where three or more hues give strong definition. The three primaries give the greatest contrast; as they become mixed as secondaries or tertiaries their strength lessens, so that red, blue and yellow are much more assertive than olive green with russet and citron. Try other schemes such as blue, red and green; or yellow, violet, red and green. With black or white added to a colour scheme, the black makes adjacent hues appear lighter but white decreases their luminosity so that they seem darker.

(b) Contrast of cool with warm colours, such as blue green with red orange. A blue green thin line on the red orange tends to 'dance', and vice versa. A red orange thin circle on the blue green background appears to move. Proportion of one colour to another is important and by experiment and with a knowledge of colour behaviour interesting colour effects can be discovered.

(c) Light and dark contrast is seen in the achromatic range of black, white and greys and in the differences between chromatic colours.

(d) Contrast of complementaries which are diametrically opposite each other in the colour circle show several different qualities. They are necessary to each other and react strongly with the complementary after images. Red orange with blue green show extremes of warm and cool colours, red and green are of equal tone values as saturated colours. Yellow and violet show extremes of light and dark contrast. All are complementary pairs of colours.

(e) Contrast of saturation, relating to the degree of purity of a colour; shows contrast between intense pure colour and diluted dull colour. The dullness may be due to a saturated colour being mixed with black, white or grey, or complementaries may be mixed. In every case they become diluted.

(f) Contrast of extension is that between a large area of colour and a small area. Although any colours may be used in any areas, certain proportions balance out one another and give better results if these are known. For example one orange:two blue; one yellow:three violet and one red : one green give good balance in theory. This is where two large, plain areas of contrasting colours have impact and stand out clearly. If these same colours are broken up into fine dots, thin lines or any small areas where the eye can merge them, the contrast is gone and the colours cancel one another out. For example fine lines or small spots of black and white appear grey together although as large solid areas they contrast boldly. Opposite hues or intensities of colour for example red+green in broken, small shapes cancel to dirty brownish grey. Analogous colours or related colours give an opposite result, such as those similar in hue or brightness, which tend to merge in adjacent areas, but diffused as optical mixtures, appear more vivid. Red with violet merge into similarity, although they may be bright, but diffused they sparkle. Blue with green produces a similar result. Blue with blue green or blue violet spots looks brilliant although large areas of each merge as one colour from a distance.

Colours of equal tone value, other than complementaries, tend to vary on the edges where they meet, for example red placed next to black gives the black edge a greenish tinge; red next to yellow makes the red slightly darker and more violet while the yellow becomes slightly green. With the pairing of colours of equal intensity this means that the complementary colour affects the edges. This reaction could be used to advantage in designs of narrow stripes, small squares and those with broken areas of two or three colours, combined with large, plain areas of the same colours. Black which reflects little light, placed next to a dark colour such as violet or blue violet, becomes tinged with the complementary colour of yellow or yellow orange and therefore makes the dark colours look brighter and lighter while the black appears browner.

If a set of one colour gradated into tones from light to dark are placed in order as wide stripes, where the stripes join one another the colours appear to be darker, thus the centres of the stripes appear lighter and give a concave effect.

Colours are inclined to be warmer or cooler according to their proximity to the red or blue areas of the colour circle but a blue can be warmer and nearer red than green, a red can be cooler and bluer than orange. This can apply to all colours and the association with temperature is useful to remember when selecting fabrics for a particular

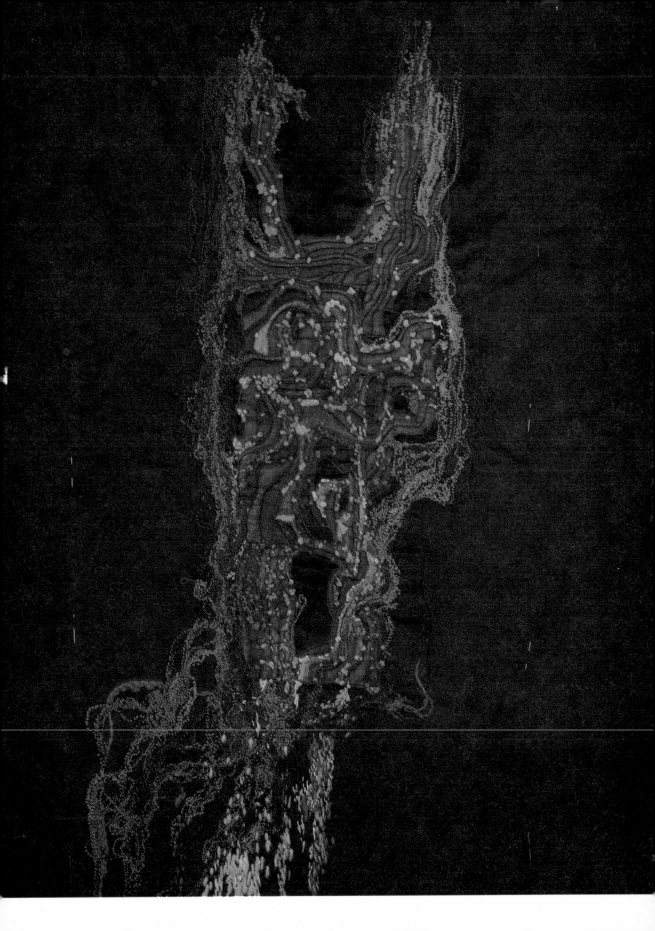

Cushion by Jeanne Abell, in black and white with the 'flesh' in pink. The striped fabric and the smaller floral pattern on white contrast strongly with the large, bold black and white patterns. Neutral tones are interesting in the use of colour, as long as there are variations in scale of patterns
Photograph by Richard Abell

purpose. Warm colours tend to excite and have more force than cool ones. Black and white can be warm or cool, black being brownish, greenish, blue-black or neutral, neither cool nor warm. White again can be creamy white or blue white, dirty white and warm or neutral. Although warm colours have a higher intensity than cool ones and normally advance, a cool, strong colour such as turquoise with a pale, warm pink, will overshadow the pink as its tonality is stronger.

When deciding upon tonal contrast light coloured shapes appear larger than dark ones and white shapes on a black ground appear to be larger than exactly similar black shapes on a white ground. Shiny surfaces as they reflect light appear stronger than dull ones. For balance in design remember to look at colour as well as shape as lighter colours appear less heavy than dark ones and a better sequence results if shapes to come forward are light, with dark ones receding. Light shapes can appear to float on dark backgrounds, especially in clear colours, as more opaque or thicker ones are again heavier. Yellow ochre is thick as compared with a light turquoise or chrome yellow; orange is thicker than sea green. Yellow on white looks darker than on black where it becomes hard and cold. Red on white becomes dark but on black looks luminous and glowing. Blue on white is dark and makes the white whiter, and on black it looks brilliant.

To separate colours of fabric into finer divisions, some colours could be sorted into warm and cold categories, some into more dense or clear colours. These can be stored

OVERLEAF *left*
Exercises on canvas 15 cm (6 in.) square by Jacqueline Mann using colours of equal value
(a) Diamonds divided into sections of analogous colours of blue green and green, with complementary colours of violet and yellow. The yellow with yellow orange arranged as a framework, appears slightly transparent. With the omission of orange red the red appears strong against the yellow
(b) The pattern is twisted to make repetition on the diagonals. The colours are broken up into

smaller areas, therefore appear more restless
(c) The diamonds are smaller, the colours concentrated into dark and light blocks. Some diamonds are divided into two analogous colours, others are in one colour. The yellows appear to float on the darker areas
(d) The diamonds are in stripes of one colour each, vertically, the horizontal stripes make bands merging from yellow, through greens and blues to purples on one side and from yellows through oranges and reds to purples on the other side

right
'Sweets' by Margaret Garner Bright red, bright green and yellow hand printed fabric which is tucked, flat and padded. The sweets are three dimensional and embroidered by hand and machine. The shadows cast by them give depth and richness to the work. The plain white area is linked to the colour with rouleaux

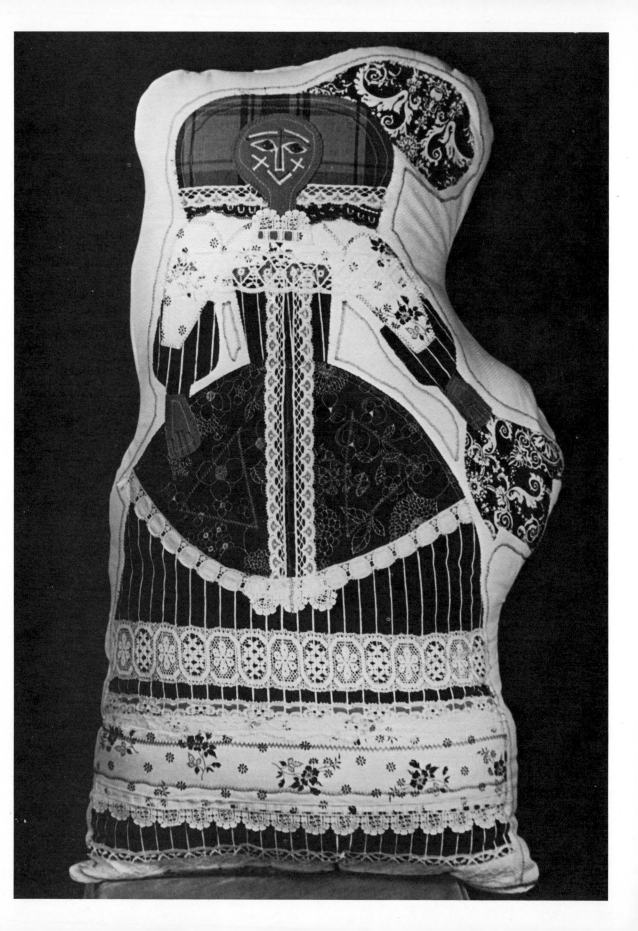

as already suggested and added to when new fabrics are acquired. They are useful for the selection of colour schemes when designing on paper.

Experiments using bright or dull complementary colours can be carried out in appliqué or stitchery or in both methods combined. Bright with dull colours, in varying proportions can be points of departure.

In paint or by matching fabrics, scales of colours between those opposite to each other can be made, such as with red at one end of the scale and green at the other and in between the mixtures of the two colours until they become grey; or orange and blue with colours gradating to grey in the centre of the scale. It would be easier to paint these colours by mixing the complementary colours in graduated proportions from the opposite ends of the scale until the equal mixture of the two produces grey, dulled colour. Then could come the interesting task of finding fabrics and threads similar to those colours mixed in paint. Any two colours mixed in varying quantities produce interesting results. Near complementaries will give surprising and often beautiful, subtle tones instead of grey or black.

Scales mixing black with pure colour and white with pure colour until these colours are darkened or made paler could also be tried, white making colours colder. From these colours mixed with pigment, fabrics can be selected to make up fabric scales. With practice it will be possible to imagine colours and their greyed images.

OVERLEAF
Colour combinations on canvas
by Pamala Whatmore
Pure colour changing to greyed
colour. The effect of stitches
worked horizontally or
vertically in one colour gives a
lighter or darker appearance.
Rearrangement of a set of
colours gives apparent change
to them.
Changing the proportion of
these colours, introducing
complementary colour, e.g. red
with green; all these factors can
be used as the basis of
experiment with one set of
colours

above
'Vanishing Point' by Madie
Lazenby, Los Altos, California
USA
Black and white appliqué, with
a stuffed and padded eyeball,
and grey wool plaids and
checks with black yarn tassels
58 cm × 142 cm (23 in. × 56 in.)
Photograph by Marion Ferri

right
Detail of 'Vanishing Point'
Grey, black and white checks
and plaids, stuffed and stitched
Photograph by Marion Ferri

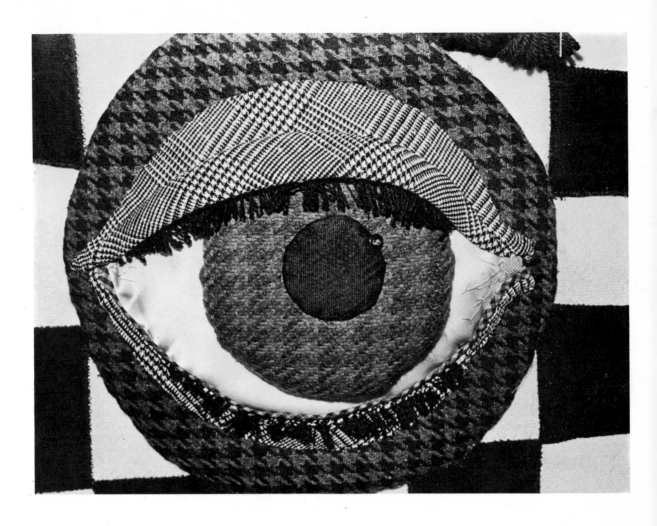

OVERLEAF *left top*
'Flower', group work by Mrs
Fidler's class of infants Southcote
Primary School, Reading
The flower made of huge petals
in fabric over cane shapes, with
buttons, beads and stitching
decorating them, is in primary
colours. It is large and exuberant.
showing enjoyment in its
creation

left bottom
'Cobweb', group work by Mrs
Edward's class, Infants Southcote
Primary School, Reading
On a large hoop, this is a group
project, in threads and crêpe
paper, in primary and other
bright colours. Ages 5–6 years.
The largest hoop available was
used as a frame, about 92 cm
(3 ft) in diameter

right
'Jewels' by Robert Burningham,
Minnesota, USA, to wear as
medallions round the neck,
hung on cords. Approximately
8–10 cm (3–4 in.). Primary
colours, beads and a variety of
threads, with spontaneous mass
use of stitches, make these small
embroideries very lively. The
shapes vary, some are padded,
the stitches cover most of the
fabric backgrounds

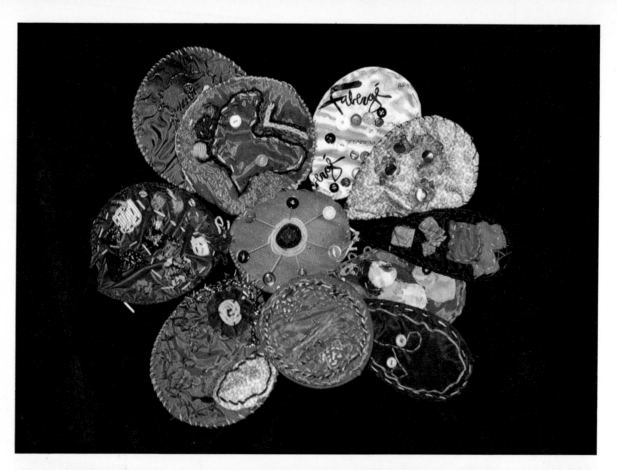

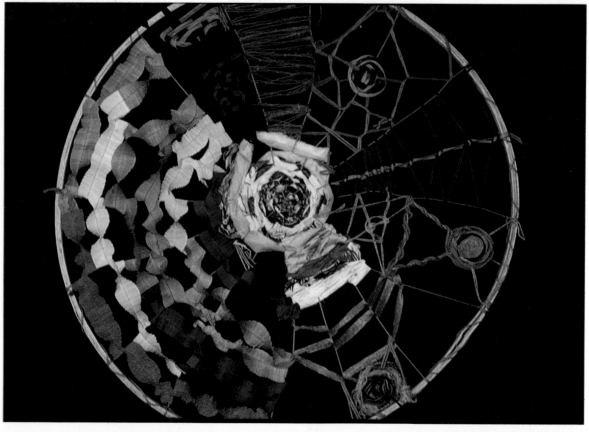

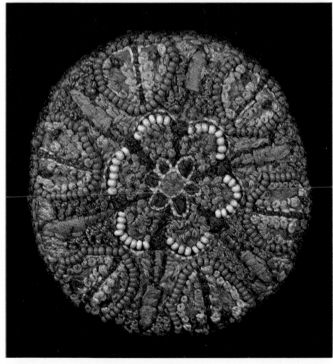

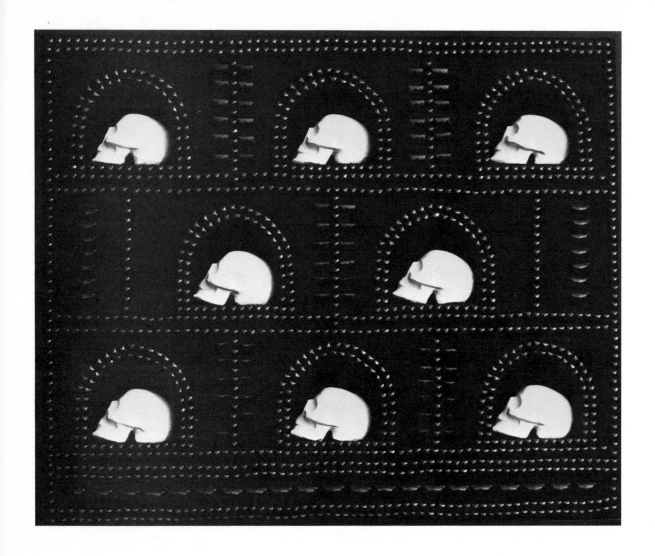

Panel by Eirian Short
Tones and textures show very
definite contrast here. The box
is in matt black fabric with
alcoves containing white plaster
skulls. Jet beads decorate the
box and stand out against the
background as they catch the
light with their shiny facetted
surfaces. The result is stark but
compelling. Approx. 107 cm ×
76 cm (3 ft 6 in. × 2 ft 6 in.)
Photograph by Denys Short

Harmony to many people means taking colours from the same circle or using tones of one colour only. Harmony means a balanced scheme of colour. Analogous colours give harmony.

One way in which to select a scheme which is harmonious is to take a pure colour, a tint and white or one or two tints and white, for example yellow, cream and pale turquoise with white.

An analogous scheme could be red, red violet and violet. Complementaries used together give harmony.

A primary colour with another primary go together and are part of what is known as a triad. This means that any three colours in a circle of equal values, that form an equilateral or isosceles triangle, are harmonious. Similarly colours from what is known as a tetrad or a shape forming a square or a rectangle, are harmonious.

Examples of a triad are red, blue and yellow; or orange, green and violet; or blue violet, yellow green and orange red.

Examples of tetrads are orange red, violet, blue green and yellow; or red, blue violet, green and orange yellow.

The equilateral triangle of colour selection – red, blue and yellow – has the highest intensity in tone.

OVERLEAF *left*
A small cushion by Lynn Harris in the primary colours of red and blue, with broken areas in seeding in red on blue and blue on red, breaking up the contours, softening the corners and merging the colours to give a purplish mixture

bottom right
'Water' by Barbara Dawson
A small panel on canvas in tapestry wools. The idea was to show two colours of equal value in large areas, diminishing to very small areas of the same two colours. The blue and red shapes are clear cut and large in the foreground, gradually becoming smaller until the two colours merge into very small stitches which from a distance appear as one violetish colour. Two colours of equal value but in contrast to each other can be effectively used in a design of large plain areas with small, broken areas of pattern. The colours will change as shapes become very small and appear to merge as a third colour. Complementary colours merge to become duller, analogous colours become more vivid
Photograph by John Hunnex

top right
Colours broken up by merging can appear as more than are actually there. Primary colours of equal value are used for this sample, but according to the scale of work and the viewing distance, optical mixtures are obtained. The red + blue becomes violetish when the stripes are narrow and of equal width, the reds + yellows become orange. As the yellow is lighter than the blue it does not merge as easily but becomes slightly green when mixed with the blue stripes
Student on short course
Photograph by John Hunnex

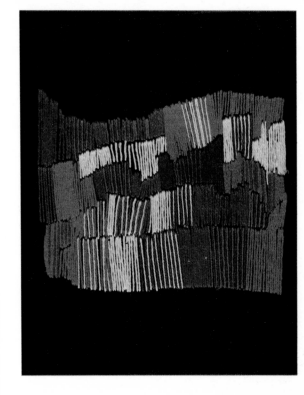

If two colours when mixed make grey in pigment, they are harmonious; they are also complementary.

Schemes of colours which are taken from different colour circles are classed sometimes as discords – in which colours are often reversed in tonal values. Schemes in this category are lively such as yellow ochre (darker than normal), lavender (lighter than normal) and olive green (darker) than in the circle of full, saturated colour. In these schemes colours are sometimes delicate, sometimes sombre with bright or clear colours as part of the choice, such as pale green, ochre and violet, pink, bright yellow and grey. Again from the collection of fabrics sorted into order, many interesting discordant colour schemes may be evolved. A scheme which is basically harmonious may be enlivened with a discordant colour such as pink (red + white) with yellow, yellow green and green. A scheme which seems equal in tone value, that is, the colours are from one circle, probably analogous and distributed fairly evenly in the design, can be given vitality by the introduction of a much darker or lighter colour or by complementary colour. A green scheme perhaps merging to blues of equal tones, although pleasant, might be more exciting with a little bright red or brilliant pink worked into it. Pale yellows with orange can be strengthened with lavender blue. Discordant colours do not make grey when mixed as pigments.

Tension Vitality and tension are created with intense warm and cool colours put together, such as bright red with turquoise blue. These colours appear to move and vibrate if a large area of red is worked with a small one of turquoise or vice versa. Warm coloured threads couched onto a cool colour, cool threads on a warm colour; bright colours on dark colour or on white all create tension, but the greatest tension of all is supposed to be a combination of brilliant red and mid-grey, which reacts with the contrast of bright green edges after a few seconds.

Intense colours always dominate weak ones, this is why it is essential to work out colour distribution, as suggested on page 207, in order to find the most successful arrangement.

These suggestions should be a point of departure only, one idea will lead to another and an effect accidentally achieved can often set off a new and exciting train of thought.

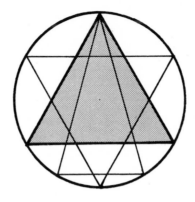

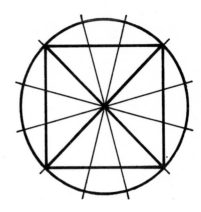

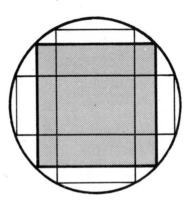

In any one circle of colours of equal value, those which make a square, a rectangle or a triangle, will harmonise with one another. The diagrams show arrangements of triangles, squares and rectangles and a circle divided into twelve segments with four colours which make a square. The triangles are called triads, the squares tetrads

OVERLEAF *left*
'Flight' by Ione Dorrington
Brilliantly coloured triangles of Thai silk appear to float on the background of purple, blue, and blue green silks all of which are shot, so that they appear to change colour when seen from different angles. Warm and cool colours are used together in this embroidery
Photograph by Ione Dorrington

right top
'Fiesta' by Helen Richards, California, USA
Colours suggest carnival, brilliant, broken into fragments; inspired by ballet – Folklorico, Mexico, with their paper streamers on headdresses.
Various stitches, on loosely woven green upholstery fabric

right bottom
'Carmina', 55 cm × 70 cm, by Wilcke Smith, New Mexico, USA
Brilliant colours are enhanced by a dark background and some padded areas. Black wool, purple detached buttonhole, padded pink shapes and long lines wrapped over threads
Photograph by Bob Smith

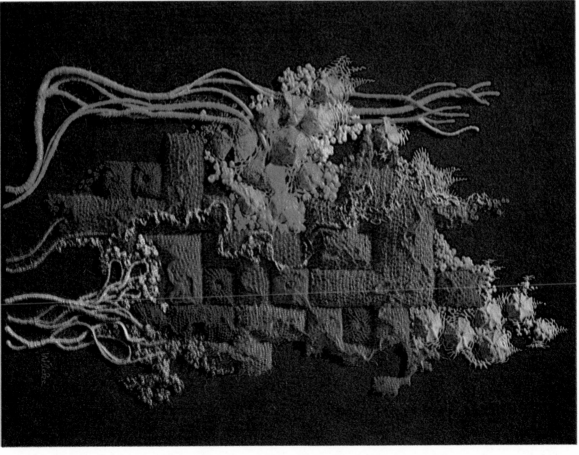

Using colour

A point to remember is that a personal use of colour can only be learnt by experiment and experience and that its use depends on the choice of the individual. Colour has physical and emotional properties. It is never seen in isolation. It is affected by many factors and is always changing.

One of the excitements of embroidery is the exploitation of colour and texture. By working stitches over areas of fabric its colour can be modified, made darker or lighter, and its texture can be altered to rougher or smoother than that of the original surface. Fine, smooth threads, thicker machine or hand spun slubbed ones, those spun with shiny and dull yarns together, those which can be separated from several strands into single strands, are among the variety available. Each has a quality suitable for particular kinds of work and types of stitches. Embroidery cannot be accomplished without background fabric or fabrics, therefore these must be chosen carefully for their purpose. With stitches worked solidly to eliminate areas of background, or worked to show the colour of the fabric between them, a metamorphosis in the surface quality, and the colour and tone of this fabric is possible. Each colour and stitch added to the work changes it and interest never flags, in fact once started, it is very difficult to put down embroidery.

It is obvious that it is necessary to collect all kinds of fabric and threads with which to experiment and from which to select basic colour schemes to express ideas. Collect coloured paper, magazine advertisements, leather, fur, woven and non-woven fabrics, ribbons, braids and other relevant materials. Keep the advertisements flat in plastic envelopes, sort out the materials at first into greens, reds, blues and yellows, then into gradations of the colours, such as bright red, then those darker and lighter than the brightest colour. From the darker and lighter colours try to pick out those which are greyed and duller from those which are clear. The colder reds can also be separated from the warmer ones. This sorting can take a great deal of time but by doing this it makes it much easier when designing, to find exactly what is wanted, also much more awareness of colour is developed. Greys can be put together and all kinds of blacks and whites, of which there are many. Large transparent plastic bags or clear plastic containers make good storage units, one for each pure colour, while the variations in the range of each colour could be kept in smaller bags within the large ones; or the small bags could be kept together in a large box labelled green, red or whatever colour is contained within it, where the whole range apart from the pure colours may be seen easily. Once sorted, whatever system is adopted it should make it quicker to find appropriate colours when needed.

To increase colour perception

(a) Choose two primary colours. Collect various tones and textures of these colours in leather, cloth, paper, etc., place pairs of equally toned colours together, whatever their textures, but of the two colours.

(b) Pair off opposite textures but equal tones of one of the colours, such as shiny with dull, rough with smooth. Here the texture will tend to make the colours more difficult to select.

(c) Arrange a whole set of one colour, in order of brightness starting from the centre and proceeding on one side to lighter colours to white and on the other to darker colours and black.

It is more difficult to arrange greyed colours and to decide between two near tones as to which is the lighter fabric. Josef Albers in his book *The Interaction of Colour* suggests a means whereby this may be determined. He says that with the two near tones 'place one colour B on top of A so that two corners overlap diagonally at C. Stare at the spot C where the two fabrics cross; remove

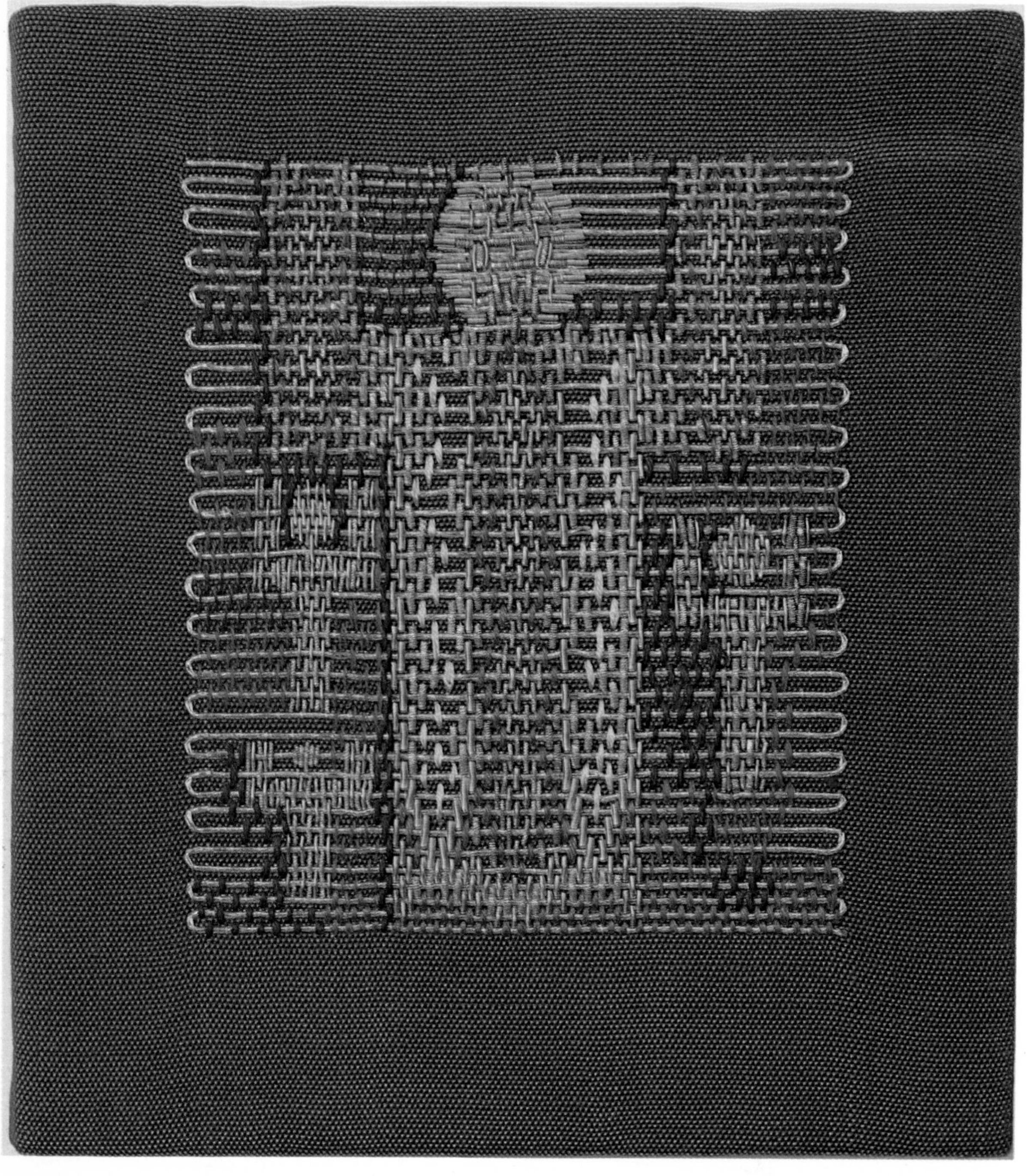

A diagram of Joseph Alber's idea for detecting the differences in tone between two near colours. See text for an explanation

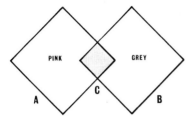

Burse 23 cm (9 in.) square by Barbara Dawson
Gold embroidery, in a free interpretation of *or nué*, the old method of couching down gold threads with coloured silks. The background is woven in blue with red, giving a pinkish purple. Four geometric figures stand out against the background, emphasised with small pieces of purl worked vertically over the horizontal gold threads which are taken completely across the square. Burden stitch in coloured silks of blue and bright pink, break up the gold of the background. This work seen from one angle looks all gold, from another only the colours show
Photograph by John Hunnex

fabric B, look quickly at the spot under C and if it looks lighter than A, the upper fabric B is darker than A. This order can be reversed to see if the result is the same.'

Try several arrangements of near tones of cloth and see which is darker by guessing, then by using Albers' experiment if unsure.

Make a number of experiments, putting two patches of one colour on slightly different coloured grounds of an equal intensity. Decide if these patches appear to change and if they do, in what way? Try a number of combinations, putting different colours on one background, the same selection of colours on different grounds. Take two colours of near intensity, juxtapose them, overlap them and place two patches apart on a ground of contrasting colour of equal intensity. Look at the three arrangements, noting any changes in the colours. Describe these, such as one colour looks greener, colder or redder and warmer when next to another; apart it looks darker/lighter. Try several colours out and 'play' with them, moving them around as much as possible. This is the best way to become aware of colour and its behaviour, and also to realise the importance of spending time on colour choice.

Exercises

1 Make a background of two near toned colours of cloth, this being in simple stripes or squares or more intricate according to skill. Work a pattern over this in one colour of thread, not too different in tone from the background. See if the colours appear to change (pinky apricot with pale orange which is more yellow, embroidered in yellow green thread).

2 Work several colours, from those near in tone to the two background colours, to darker and lighter ones such as medium turquoise and very pale grey together. The effect should be richer, with more depth.

3 Try appliqué using two opposite textures of cloth designed to make a counterchange. A suggestion is to use velvet and wool, satin or silk and cotton. Apply velvet to the wool and vice versa for the complete design, or satin to the cotton and vice versa. Stitches in different kinds of thread but the same colours as those of the fabrics added to this idea in reversing materials, can result in an intricate embroidery.

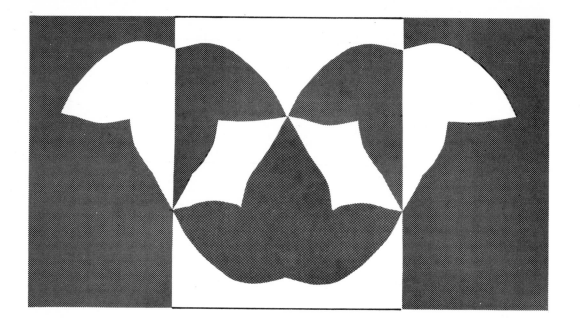

To obtain colour samples

Before deciding on those colours required in an embroidery, preliminary exercises can be tried which are added to indefinitely. They are valuable for reference at any time and by varying the proportions of colours used and by incorporating different textures, ideas can be developed entirely from them. Card strips about 30 cm × 5 cm (12 in. × 2 in.) are wound with threads of different colours and textures, in varying proportions of stripe. By this means, colours which react strongly to one another, those which do not go together, those which are pleasing and those which are exciting and vibrant when combined, can be judged. The card may be covered with the background fabric already chosen for an embroidery, the threads being wound over this.

Exercises

1   Wind in tapestry wool the three primary colours, red, blue and yellow, to make different widths of stripe, combining them in different orders.

2   Wind the secondary colours similarly.

3   Put primary colours and secondary colours together.

4   Select dark colours, winding them in varying proportions, for example, indigo, dark brown and slate grey; crimson, purple and olive green.

Simple counterchange. Light on dark and dark on light fabric. This pattern can be repeated in several ways. Counterchange is effective on a bold scale, using two colours of near tones for a 'quiet' result; two colours which contrast strongly, for a 'striking' result

5   Select tints such as pale blue, lemon and white, or pale silvery grey, pale, warm pink and apricot and wind them to make interesting combinations of stripe.

6   Use darker and paler colours together.

7   Wind colours already used but change the types of thread if possible. Note differences in the first exercises and these. Find out which ones are preferred, with reasons for the choice.

8   Wind a colour scheme that vibrates, one that is calm and subtle and one that looks harsh and unsympathetic. Analyse the reasons for the selection of colours.

For reference, coloured advertisements can be cut up and graded in order of tones, from light to dark. Stick down squares of colour on black or white paper, trying to obtain as near gradations as possible. These scales are useful when choosing fabrics and in mixing colours on paper for design.

To show the effect of a background colour on a design (a) On three 125 mm (5 in.) squares in three different colours of fabric; for example, grey, bright pink and turquoise, make a pattern in one colour of thread only such as bright blue. This pattern should be reasonably similar in each instance. Note any differences in the apparent colour of the embroidery on the different grounds. (b) Work the same pattern on a white background and on a black background, using the same colour of thread as in (a).

A design can be changed entirely by altering the background colour, for better or worse. A student worked out a design on paper, in scarlet on white, and wishing to carry it out in embroidery went to buy a suitable material. She came back with a bright green, shiny fabric and proceeded to embroider the design in red. Half way through she realised that what she was doing was not what she had intended and it took her some time to realise that the background was different. The result she obtained was more exciting than the original idea, as the red and the green being complementary to each other vibrated in the solid areas of stem stitch and merged into browns in the areas in which seeding was worked on the green.

Colour and tone

Exercises

1 Choose a neutral background fabric – grey, black or white – about 20 cm (8 in.) square. Embroider or apply two stripes of fabric about 25 mm (1 in.) wide in one colour, preferably a clear, bright hue such as a mid blue, work the background in gradated tones of one contrasting colour, perhaps a dark, dull red gradating from a pale, dusty pink at the top of the square to as dark a colour as possible at the bottom. Dye white thread if insufficient colours are available as at least five tones will be needed for them to be effective. Work small stitches such as seeding, french or chinese knots or work rows of running stitches across the square in horizontal lines to make a close texture or merging tones. The gradated background will appear to change the depth of colour of the stripes, which will look darker at the top on the lighter stitching and lighter at the bottom on the darker coloured stitching.

On a large scale this experiment is better accomplished by dip dying a background fabric so that it goes from a light to a dark colour. A simple pattern on this dyed fabric can be worked closely in one colour with machine stiching, such as in rows of adjacent satin stitch or in an even, all-over texture of free stitching, or by hand in any suitable stitches; or a pattern may be applied in another, plain coloured fabric. Again, the apparent change in the colour of the pattern will be seen.

2 Work the background entirely, leaving the pattern in the fabric. Mark out a design on a mid-grey fabric, work the background in several tones of one colour, in couched threads or in long running stitches, or in darning according to the intricacy of the pattern. Each of several ways the background may be worked will give different results.

(a) Work from the centre of the design across to the vertical edges, with vertical rows of stitches, light in the centre to dark outside.

(b) Reverse the process and start with the darkest colour in the centre.

(c) Work from the top to the bottom of the design using light threads going to dark ones and vice versa.

(d) Work the background in stripes of different colours of equal intensity.

The grey pattern will appear to change in colour according to the colours behind it.

Diagrams to show the distribution of stitching on a background, in some of the suggestions leaving the pattern in the fabric only. Other ideas show both pattern and background work, but reversing the order of colours or tones. The ideas can be carried out in darning patterns, running, solid line stitches such as couching, stem, backstitch. Colours can merge from dark to light, from dull to bright. Lines can be placed very closely together to far apart. A different arrangement of colours and spaces changes an idea completely as does the shifting of the weights and textures of threads. The change in scale of an embroidery also requires a reassessment of weights of thread and ways of working out the designs

3   Mark out on a brightly coloured or strongly toned fabric, a series of simple shapes which are spaced about 6 mm ($\frac{1}{4}$ in.) apart and are fairly equal in size. The kind of pattern and the weight of threads chosen depends on the scale of the work but there should be gradated colours available whatever colours of thread are used for the stitches, or white through a range of greys to black, to show the point of the exercise.

(a) Work from the top of the horizontal edge of the fabric to the bottom, surrounding the shapes in the lightest colour on the top row, mingling the lightest with the next tone on the next horizontal row, gradually working to the bottom edge of the fabric where the shapes will be surrounded with the darkest colour available. Keep the lighter colour next to the shape in each instance and judge the number of rows round each shape according to scale.

(b) Work a similar idea out, but start from the centre of the fabric or from the outside edges of the fabric working to the centre, gradating the colour from light to dark, from whichever point is chosen as a beginning. The colours of the shapes will appear to change in tone according to whether they are surrounded by light or dark colour.

From this exercise it follows that apparent depth may be created by working within a shape such as a circle, with strong colours merging to light colours round the outer edge, or with a dark colour round the outer edge to light in the centre.

This again leads to an embroidery which could appear to be lit with a spotlight. If the complete piece of work is embroidered in dark colours and one small area is worked in light, more yellow colours, with fairly well defined edges, the effect is of a light directed to that area.

To find out the reaction of colours to background

(a) Place different coloured shapes on a black background or closely work a design in a variety of coloured threads. Carry out exactly the same procedure on a white background and note the difference between the two pieces of work.

It will be found that near tones sink into the background while, strongly contrasting ones come forward.

On a background of stripes in crimson, violet red, greyed violet red and blue violet, a very bright ultramarine blue thread was used to work spots of colour in vertical lines such as couching, stem stitch or back stitch. The colours appeared to sink or advance in parts and the following observations were made: on the crimson the blue was intense and strong; on the violet red the blue looked less intense and receded slightly; on the greyed violet red the blue was again stronger but looked duller; and on the blue violet the blue stitching almost disappeared.

Again using bright emerald green threads and working solid shapes on a background of dark olive green, bright blue and lighter grey blue; the green on the olive green looked dark and intense, on the bright blue it looked brighter and lighter and on the greyed blue it looked darker but duller than on the bright blue.

Using threads of the same green, work on to a red ground of equal intensity, a pattern of different sized shapes, the small ones nearer to one another, the large more separate with space between. From a distance the small spots will appear to merge with the ground but the large ones will stand out. An explanation of this will be found in the chapter on colour theory, page 166.

Density of stitches

1   Work french knots very closely to scattered. Use one colour of tapestry wool and crewel wool on a mid-grey ground, making large knots with double twists, in the thicker wool, to small knots with one twist in the thinner wool, scattering the small ones until they appear to fade away.

2   Work hungarian or roumanian couching horizontally and vertically in rectangular/square blocks. Space the rows to show unequal stripes of background fabric. Use thread appropriate to the scale of the work, and in a colour darker or lighter than that of the ground chosen.

3   Work a similar exercise using two colours of thread of equal intensity, complementary or analogous, mixing

them and varying the distances between the couched lines. If complementary colours are chosen they will appear to merge where the lines are closer together and will look dull. If the colours are analogous they will appear brighter together.

Optical mixing

The mixing of two colours visually, seen simultaneously by the eye so that they merge to make one colour was practised by the Impressionists in the last century.

This intermingling is called optical mixing and is the basis of colour printing, where screens of very fine dots are overprinted to give other colours. This is a way in which stitches may be used to advantage, working with two or more colours of equal depth, in small dots. From a distance the dots of colour will appear to merge and will give the effect of mixtures of the colours.

The French artist Seurat (1859–91) developed a method of painting in small dots of pure colour which became known as 'pointillism'. Instead of mixing pigments as had been practised previously, his use of pure colour was intended to create more luminosity and from a distance these dots did give this quality.

Exercises

A neutral ground of black, grey or white is necessary as a starting point, although when worked over, the background will show through the stitches very little. After trying one or two ideas, backgrounds of any colour can be chosen. These exercises are only a beginning as the permutations of colours are endless. The colours should be of equal intensity to give a good mixture.

1   On a white ground work a closely knit area of stitches such as french knots, link chain, seeding or loops, in two primary colours of thread, preferably thick, such as soft cotton or no. 3 perle and combining the right colours. Red + blue will look violet from a distance, red + yellow will look orange, blue + yellow will look green.

2   Try narrow stripes in two colours, combined with plain areas of each of the colours.

3   Dotted stitches and smooth stitches may be incorporated in a pattern of checks, using two colours of thread on a neutral ground. Blue and red dots, a plain blue, blue

G G+R R R+B B B+Y Y

Merging of two colours of thread to make a third colour, may be done here with lines of thread or stitches. The diagram shows a simple exercise where G = green + R = red are merged. These two colours will appear duller and brownish grey at G + R. Red + B = blue, may make a merged colour of a dull brownish blue or a clearer, purplish colour, according to the kinds of red and blue merged. Vermilion and cold blue make a greyish brown colour, but crimson and a very bright warm blue give a purplish mixture. Blue + Y = yellow give green. Again the blue is cold, such as prussian blue and the yellow is clear like chrome or lemon, combined the green is clear; but ultramarine or cobalt with gamboge give a duller green. This exercise could develop into a complicated pattern of merging colours in threads of different textures

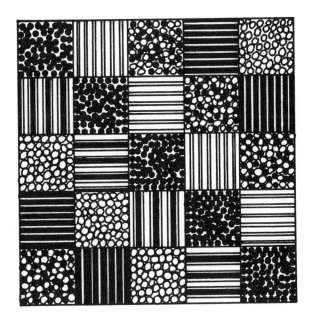

RED

BLUE

RED
+ BLUE

A pattern of spots and stripes, in which two colours of equal tone value may be combined to make a third colour in some of the squares. From a distance and according to the scale of this idea, colours will appear to merge when mixed in one square

The key indicates the distribution of the colours which have been selected as carmine red and ultramarine blue in this instance. After trying out primary colours much more subtle ones may be substituted, from a range of equal tone values. More complicated patterns using more than two colours can be devised from this beginning

and red dots then a plain red makes a series of checks which can be repeated to make an interesting permutation; worked out as A = dots, B = plain blue, A = dots, D = plain red. In a 16 square pattern, the next horizontal block of squares read B = blue, A = dots, D = red, A = dots etc. Various arrangements of squares and colours can be worked out in sequences, to give really complicated colour changes. Try the simple ones first of all and if a large scale work is contemplated, use appliqué and stitchery together.

4   Use several colours of equal intensity, working small samples of the mixtures together with plain areas of each of the colours. Note the results. Find out why some combinations of colour are more successful than others and whether the types of thread and stitch chosen has affected the results. After practice with the more obvious colours, try the more subtle ones.

Transparency

Optical mixing of colours can produce an effect of transparency without using transparent fabrics, by using colours of equal value, tones of a colour and mixtures of those colours. Josef Albers suggests one way of showing this transparency, which can be done by taking colour A and colour B plus the mixture of the two colours. It is easier to choose the primary colours before embarking on the more subtle schemes. Take red and yellow which when mixed make orange. Cut three equal rectangles in paper or fabric, one red, one yellow and one orange, of equal value. Place the red rectangle horizontally, with the orange one vertically to overlap the red, for less than half its width and about central along its length. Place the yellow rectangle over the orange one, vertically, but with its top edge level with the bottom of the red edge. If the orange rectangle is in between the red and the yellow in colour it should appear translucent. If interesting results are to be obtained mix subtle colours in paint then try to obtain them in fabrics, keeping the 'mixed' areas larger than those from which the mixture results.

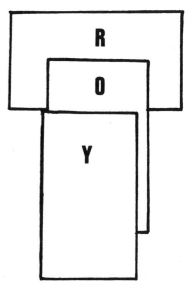

   Tissue paper and sheer fabrics are useful in ascertaining what happens to colours when mixed, as by overlapping two tissue papers or by placing a transparent fabric over a brightly coloured opaque one, in each case a third colour results. The two overlapping colours put together with the

Each diagram shows an idea whereby an apparent feeling of transparency is obtained with opaque colours of equal intensity

An exercise
W = a white background on which one blue stripe = B and one red stripe = R are applied fabrics, the blue being bright but not cold, the red being scarlet and not crimson or vermilion. Bright yellow thread is worked as a stripe over the white, in a stitch such as satin, but over the colours an equal amount of the background colour shows in between the threads, to give a mixture; on the blue background + the yellow thread = green, and on the red background + yellow thread = orange. According to the scale of the pattern the choice and the thickness of threads are important

Here, small dots or french knots are worked in a lighter red than the crimson fabric. Where they are worked over the crimson, that area looks slightly transparent as it appears lighter

Blue fabric is applied to the white stripes, violet fabric is applied to the red stripe, green fabric is applied to the yellow stripe. Throughout the exercises, the colours must be of equal value, therefore it is easier to practise with the more obvious ones before trying to use the more subtle colours.
If transparent white fabric is placed over a bright colour, it becomes paler. On the bright colour work an area of close stitching in the paler colour, as near to the whitened one as possible. This will give an appearance of transparency on the bright fabric. The bright colour can be overlaid with black transparent fabric, then the darker result can be matched in threads which are worked closely together on the bright colour. Exercises may be devised to give a variety of simulated transparency

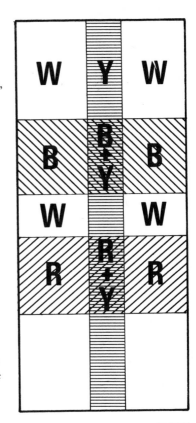

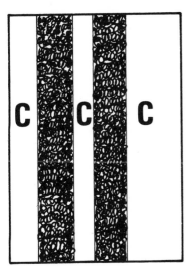

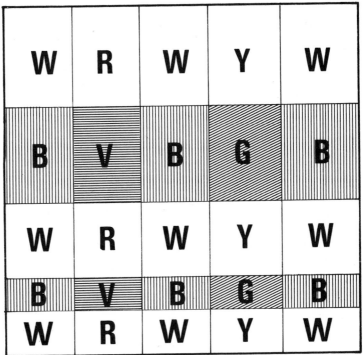

third colour made by the overlapping, in the right order, will produce apparent transparency using opaque fabrics. An example is to take black nylon organza, place it over bright red, so that a bronzish colour is made, double the organza and the bronze becomes darker. Find opaque fabrics to match the different bronzes then use the bright red fabric plus the bronze in sequence and an effect of transparency is obtained.

Another effect of transparency is obtained by using tones of one colour, such as a fabric of a pure colour with the same colour mixed with black which results in a darker colour and the pure colour mixed with white which results in a paler colour. Canvas stitchery can be used to good effect in this way, with florentine stitch or any stitch which gives smooth gradations of colour.

An exercise using primary colours as a test before embroidering on more subtle schemes is to apply to a piece of white fabric two stripes, approximately 30 mm ($1\frac{1}{4}$ in.) wide in different primary colours of fabric of a similar texture. Allow about 50 mm (2 in.) on either side of the stripes and about 25 mm (1 in.) between them, although this is arbitrary as long as they are spaced apart. Thread of the third primary colour is worked as a pattern to cross the white fabric and the coloured stripes. This may consist of another stripe, an initial letter or any suitable shape, worked in close stem or chain stitch. If the stripes chosen are red and blue, yellow thread is stitched on the white fabric but where the pattern crosses the red stripe it is worked in orange thread of an equal intensity, and again, where it crosses the blue stripe a green thread of the same intensity is used, as red plus yellow makes orange and blue plus yellow makes green. French knots may be substituted for the chain or stem stitch, working them closely on the white ground. Where they cross the coloured stripes space the stitches to show an equal amount of colour and stitch. The bright yellow thread on red fabric will appear orange, and on the blue fabric a green colour will result. The effect, more pronounced from a distance, will appear to be transparent. Fabrics may be substituted for threads where the pattern crosses the stripes. In this particular case orange fabric and green fabric patches of equal intensity could be applied to or inlet into the stripes while yellow fabric could be applied to the white. This is an idea for patchwork using primary colours and those made by mixing them.

The design would have to be planned so that two shapes in primary colours would contain between these, a third shape in a mixture of the colours. Neutral colours with these would be useful in separating areas of strong colour. Small areas of pattern in apparently transparent colour in an otherwise opaque scheme could make an effective bedspread, working in applied fabrics and stitches.

Direction of stitch

The direction in which some stitches are worked affects their tones, sometimes they look darker, sometimes lighter than their actual colour. This can be exploited in an embroidery carried out entirely in one stitch.

Exercises

1   On a plain background, in a lighter or darker coloured thread work small blobs or spots, approximately 12 mm to 19 mm ($\frac{1}{2}$ in. to $\frac{3}{4}$ in.), in close cretan or satin stitch. Space these blobs unevenly, working them at different angles to catch the light. They have an up and down movement, but in the next exercise the movement is circular in working the spots.

2   Work small woven, knotted and back stitched wheels, unevenly spaced but with some sort of rhythm behind the pattern.

3   Plan a pattern of larger spots, about 19 mm ($\frac{3}{4}$ in.) across. Work some of these spots in spirals, in stem, chain or twisted chain, very closely stitched. Work other spots vertically and/or horizontally in closely touching straight lines. Keep to one colour of thread and distribute the different textures to give interesting tonal results.

4   Work small patterns using shiny threads in self-colour, in chain, stem, fishbone and any suitable stitches. Vary the spacing of lines and shapes to give closely worked and more openly worked areas.

By varying the direction of long lines of threads, sewn diagonally and loosely, to create slight shadows, movement is obtained, but threads freely attached are suitable only for embroideries which are not handled. Long threads caught lightly to the background fabric, taken diagonally over one another, sometimes just off the vertical, sometimes at angles up to 45° to the vertical can also give movement. When they become massed by overlapping, colour becomes intense and if colours and textures of threads are chosen to emphasise this effect, exercises using groups of colours are worth experiment.

1   Use mainly one range of colour, such as red or blue, streaked with one or two threads of brilliant emerald green or orange pink.

2   Use dull colours with pure, saturated colours, such as greyed greens and yellows with intense blue or scarlet.

Lines worked diagonally over fabric with narrow stripes can produce a flickering movement, especially if worked in fan like directions as in the sun's rays.

Proportions of colours in a design

Proportions of colours in a design are important and by changing the sequence of tones and colours, the final result can be completely altered. The amount of a particular colour and its placement in relation to other colours in a composition, gives different results if

(a) the proportion of a particular colour is changed, e.g., more red and less blue is substituted for more blue and less red;

(b) the colours are rearranged in another sequence so that the reaction of one on another is different, e.g., red is placed next to mid-grey and violet, instead of next to pale blue and yellow ochre;

(c) the tones are shifted so that the weights of colour are altered, eg, where red was placed originally, pale blue is substituted.

To realise this it is better to work with fabrics and threads, as surface qualities of texture and stitches worked on the fabrics give a different effect from that of using one texture of paper. Small fabric collages are the most accurate way of demonstrating these points but to start with, preliminary exercises in colour shifting are more quickly accomplished with paint, coloured pencils, cut or torn paper. Once the principles involved are mastered, then return to fabrics which are more precious and not to be wasted. For the experiments using paper, trace out a design five or six times onto white paper. Choose the number of colours required, arranging them differently

Six examples of a design, in which the three tones are distributed differently in each. A number of small shapes are contained in the design, which can become confused or simplified according to the placing of the tones. The tones may represent more than three colours as different ones may be of equal value, such as a dark red and a purple together, or an olive green and a brown and a dark grey. Three light tones of equal value such as pale pink, pale grey and lemon yellow may be represented in the diagrams by the white areas. Decide which one, if any, is more successful than another then try your own arrangement in neutral colours of the three tones, in preference to the illustrations. Analyse your efforts, then translate one design into colour

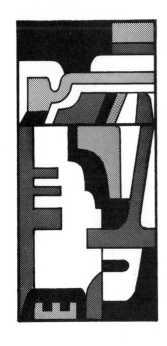

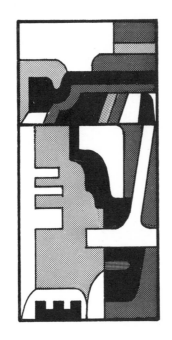

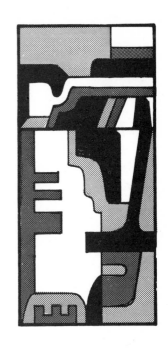

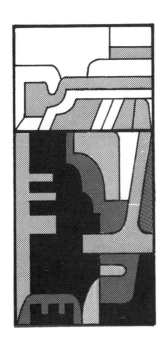

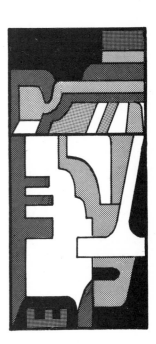

in each tracing, either by painting, drawing or by using paper shapes. Select the result that is most satisfactory and the worst one, trying to see why one works, the other does not. If the result looks spotty this is probably due to dark and light tones being scattered with few intermediate ones in between; the contrast is too sudden and the grouping of tones in some sort of order, has been omitted. If the tones are arranged as dark, medium and light, the result is less spotty than if they are in the order of dark, light and medium where there is a break in continuity. A pattern in tones of colour in sequence seems more coherent than one in which they are out of order, appearing restless.

If the result looks dull in parts this may be due to equal tones being placed together so that they merge into less interesting shapes. There can be too little or too much of one colour, too many colours used for the size of the design, or too little or too much equality of tone.

If a large number of colours is being used in a design, a scheme tending to the warm side or the cool side will give better results than if there is no plan. To co-ordinate tones in a design, these can be painted in on tracings, in black, greys and white. When a satisfactory distribution is reached, colours of similar tone values can be exchanged for the neutrals, by superimposing coloured papers over the painted shapes.

An exercise which involves additions of colour and therefore changes the proportions, is interesting but takes time to carry out. Design a small motif, or whatever is wished, working.
(a) the complete idea entirely in outline, in one colour on a darker or lighter ground;
(b) work as for (a) but introducing another colour to fill in and emphasise parts of the design;
(c) work as for (b) but again add another colour and if necessary continue this procedure until the embroidery is complete. According to its size this may make up to six small embroideries or more.

The uses of stripes of thread and fabric mentioned on page 194 are a help in deciding proportions of colour for a design. Stripes in grey, black and white in contrast to those in near tones of grey will show the difference between using very near toned colours which lack vitality and in using strongly contrasting colours modified by medium tones.

By making a viewer, a part of a drawing, design or photograph may be isolated from the whole. In this way interesting small areas can be selected and enlarged, as completely new designs, whereas they might not have been picked out just by looking at the whole illustration rather perfunctorarily.

In the examples drawn, some of the selected parts give compositions which might be seen upside down or turned to one side, or combined with other shapes

Dark colours at the bottom of a design tend to make it heavy but wherever the concentration of interest is intended in a design, there the colour should be in greater contrast to the rest of the area. For example pale pink and orange clouds in the background of a panel, floating from the bottom upwards, with darker and more strongly coloured figures concentrated towards the top right hand corner give a dynamic quality to an idea based on the 'Valkyrie' by Richard Box, in which figures float up to heaven against a delicate atmospheric array of chiffons in pale colours. The panel by Kay Macklam in which bright, paler colours are concentrated in the centre, giving the appearance of light, also looks strongly three dimensional. This is due partly to the direction in which the stitches are worked, partly to the dark colours against the light, giving the appearance of shadows made by threaded fabrics. Actually the panel is stitched entirely, without any padding.

Bright, light colours will bring shapes forward as against greyer shapes which tend to appear as further away. As already stated on page 171, warm colours usually advance but can appear heavy while cool ones recede but can appear thin. This order can be changed with the intensity of a colour which means that a strong turquoise blue can overshadow a pale orange or apricot.

An unrelated colour in a scheme of work can mar the complete result but if the colours are worked out before the embroidery is started this saves a great deal of trouble. If it is difficult to find which colour is wrong, mask out in the collage or in the painted design each area of colour separately, or place other coloured paper shapes over those already painted. If the embroidery has been worked spontaneously but does not appear quite satisfactory and it still seems to be unco-ordinated, try working in thread with one of the dominant colours, over another area, to 'pull the colour across' as it were. If a colour is too bright or too dull it can be changed with more stitching over it, to darken or lighten, to dull or to make brighter. Threads can be laid down before actual stitching takes place if there is uncertainty about the placing of the colour. The textures of these can give different effects, according to their dull or shiny appearance as well as their thickness and roughness or smoothness.

Unity can be obtained by looking at an embroidery through a piece of coloured cinemoid. This acts as a

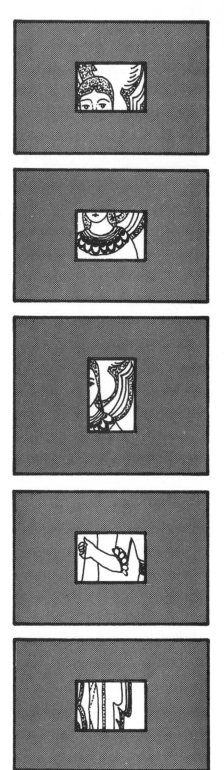

filter, reducing the colours to tones also gives similar results to the mixing of one colour with all the colours in a design, so co-ordinating them. Some colours appear to sink, some will come forward, they may be spotty, but more threads can be worked into these areas to give greater balance to the tones until the embroidery is satisfactory. A viewer can be made with a small hole cut in a large piece of paper, through which the embroidery may be looked at in small concentrated sections. This is a help in finding unsatisfactory colours and tones in different areas so that they can be altered. It is also useful in design where small, interesting areas can be picked out from real objects, photographs, drawings or paintings, and patterns. The viewer is a means of isolating these parts for different purposes, such as the finding of textures, colours or shapes, any of which can be utilized in embroidery. Without it the particular examples might not have been recognised as potential ideas for design.

Suppliers

GREAT BRITAIN

Embroidery threads and accessories. Many stock fabrics, beads and sequins, and gold and silver kid as well

Mrs Mary Allen
Turnditch, Derbyshire

E J Arnold and Son Limited
(School Suppliers)
Butterley Street
Leeds LS10 1AX

Art Needlework Industries
Limited
7 St Michael's Mansions
Ship Street
Oxford OX1 3DG

The Campden Needlecraft
Centre
High Street
Chipping Campden
Gloucestershire

Craftsman's Mark Limited
Broadlands, Shortheath
Farnham, Surrey

Dryad (Reeves) Limited
Northgates
Leicester LE1 4QR

B Francis
4 Glenworth Street
London NW1

Fresew
97 The Paddocks
Stevenage
Herts SG2 9UQ

Louis Grossé Limited
36 Manchester Street
London W1 5PE

Handweavers Studio
29 Haroldstone Road
Walthamstow
London E17 7AN

The Handworkers' Market
8 Fish Hill
Holt, Norfolk

Harrods Limited
London W1

Thomas Hunter Limited
56 Northumberland Street
Newcastle upon Tyne
NE1 7DS

Levencrafts
54 Church Square
Guisborough, Cleveland

Mace and Nairn
89 Crane Street
Salisbury, Wiltshire SP1 2PY

MacCulloch and Wallis
Limited
25–26 Dering Street
London W1R 0BH

The Needlewoman Shop
146–148 Regent Street
London W1R 6BA

Nottingham Handcraft
Company
(School Suppliers)
Melton Road
West Bridgford
Nottingham

Christine Riley
53 Barclay Street
Stonehaven
Kincardineshire AB3 2AR

Royal School of Needlework
25 Princes Gate
Kensington SW7 1QE

The Silver Thimble
33 Gay Street
Bath

J Henry Smith Limited
Park Road, Calverton
Woodborough
nr Nottingham

Elizabeth Tracy
45 High Street
Haslemere, Surrey

Mrs Joan L Trickett
110 Marsden Road
Burnley, Lancashire

Wippell Mowbray
Church Furnishings Ltd
1 Cathedral Yard
Exeter EX4 3DW
also at
11 Tufton Street
London SW1P 3QB
and
24 King Street
Manchester M2 6HG

Beads and sequins

Sesame Ventures
Greenham Hall
Wellington, Somerset

Ells and Farrier Ltd
5 Princes Street
London W1R 8PH

Leather, gold and silver kid

The Light Leather Group
Alpha House, The Hyde
Edgware Road
London NW9 5EB

Suede and leather offcuts

Redpath Campbell and
Partners Limited
Department CH13
Cheapside
Stroud, Gloucestershire

John P Milner Ltd
67 Queen Street
Hitchin, Herts

USA

Embroidery threads and accessories

Appleton Brothers of London
West Main Road
Little Compton
Rhode Island 02837

American Crewel Studio
Box 553 Westfield
New Jersey 07091

American Thread
Corporation
90 Park Avenue
New York

Bucky King Embroideries
Unlimited
Box 124c, King Bros
3 Ranch, Buffalo Star Rkc
Sheriden
Wyoming 82801

Casa de las Tejedoras
1618 East Edinger
Santa Ana
California 92705

Colonial Textiles
2604 Cranbrook
Ann Arbor
Michigan 48104

Craft Kaleidoscope
6412 Ferguson Street
Indianapolis 46220

Dharma Trading Company
1952 University Avenue
Berkeley
California 94704

Folklorico Yarn Co
522 Ramona Street
Palo Alto 94301
California

The Golden Eye
Box 205
Chestnut Hill
Massachusetts 02167

Heads and Tails
River Forest
Illinois 60305

Leonida Leatherdale
Embroidery Studio
90 East Gate
Winnipeg,
Manitoba R3C 2C3
Canada

Lily Mills
Shelby
North Carolina 28150

The Needle's Point Studio
7013 Duncraig Court
McLean
Virginia 22101

Sutton Yarns
2054 Yonge Street
Toronto 315
Ontario, Canada

Threadbenders
2260 Como Avenue
St Paul, Minnesota 55108

The Thread Shed
307 Freeport Road
Pittsburgh
Pennsylvania 15215

Yarn Bazaar
Yarncrafts Limited
3146 M Street
North West Washington DC

Yarn Depot
545 Sutter Street
San Francisco 94118
California

Leather, gold and silver kid

Aerolyn Fabrics Inc
380 Broadway
New York

Index